WORD OF TRUTH CATECHISM

M. J. Kirstine

ISBN-10: 0692934715
ISBN-13: 978-0692934715 (Proper Thought)

Be diligent to present yourself
approved to God as a workman who
does not need to be ashamed,
accurately handling the word of truth.
2 Timothy 2:15 (NASB)

Table of Contents

Table of Contents - Continued

Table of Contents - Continued

Table of Contents - Continued

Table of Contents - Continued

Acknowledgements

First and foremost, all glory and honor to God. That He would lavishly pour out saving and sanctifying grace on an undeserving sinner like me is beyond amazing. Without His work in my life, I have no ability to produce a catechism like this.

I am also blessed by God's gift of solid fellowship in the community of believers.
I am very appreciative for the several brothers in Christ who have given insight and attention to help refine this catechism. Without their suggestions, this work would not be what it is today.
The amount of time and focus that went into clean-up edits by a wonderful sister in Christ will never be forgotten. I cannot say, "Thank you," enough.
And through the long production process, my precious wife has joyfully given herself to all that God has for her as wife and mother, providing me the opportunity to take on this writing task. I love you sweetheart.

Introduction

Catechize *(verb)* [**Catechizing** *(present participle)*]:
To instruct someone in biblical truths by means of question
and answer, using a catechism.

A Christian catechism is designed to help believers understand
biblical truths, spot theological error, be able to give a defense
for the hope that is in us, and grow in holiness. The Apostle
Paul wrote in 2 Timothy 2:15, "Be diligent to present yourself
approved to God as a workman who does not need to be
ashamed, accurately handling the word of truth" (NASB). The
diligence encouraged in this passage is one all Christians
should have. In our modern times, this is as important as ever;
far too many professing Christians lack knowing and putting
into practice sound doctrine. For some, the very idea of
focusing on growing in these ways is foreign or seems
overwhelming, but that does not have to be the case. In this
catechism, you'll find short questions and answer responses,
biblical references for seeing the doctrine taught in God's
word, and additional points and definitions.

It is often assumed that the use of a catechism is a Roman
Catholic invention. This, however, is not accurate. There is
much proof of the early Christian Church utilizing catechism,
all the way through the Reformation and onward. It is widely
known that theologians such as Augustine of Hippo, John
Calvin, John Owen, Benjamin Keach, Charles Spurgeon, and
Arthur W. Pink benefited from and ministered with Christian
catechisms. Several important catechisms throughout Church
history have been written and used: *The Westminster Larger and
Shorter Catechism, The Heidelberg Catechism,* and *Keach's
Catechism* are a few. Returning to the time-tested practice of
catechizing is a proven way to grow without being
overwhelmed. Now, even a great catechism cannot and should
not replace the New Testament command to be a part of a
sound, local church to be fully discipled and to sit under sound

preaching and teaching by qualified elders. But adding a catechism to use in the context of the local church and at home is quite a blessing. The use of catechisms in this way is what we see when we look back in Christian Church history. Unfortunately, for many contemporary Christians, the idea of catechizing is largely a foreign concept.

With such a rich history and proven testimony, it was my desire to take part in using a catechism in my home and the local church where I serve as an elder. But as good as the historic catechisms are, it seemed to me that having a catechism with both modern English language *and* the historic Christian truths would be most beneficial. So, I set out to produce what you are now holding. In this process, I thought it best to lean on many existing resources in this work. Along with my own writing, in this catechism you'll find language from the 1689 Confession of Faith and some familiar language from other recent writings and historic catechisms. Like the Baptist Confession's nod to the Westminster Confession, utilizing other resources in producing this work is my attempt to show respect to and orthodoxy with biblical theologians, in this case, from a vast spectrum of centuries.

For believers, there are many benefits in using and memorizing a catechism. The primary three are:

1) Catechizing will help you understand and know sound doctrine. The questions' answers are short doctrinal statements, and the Scripture support references will help affirm the biblical teaching and show you where to find it. When used in the context of a local church, a catechism has many significant benefits, the primary being that the catechism can help the members of the church be doctrinally unified.

2) Catechizing helps us grow in apologetics. Apologetics is defined as *a defense of the Christian faith*. Voddie Baucham said the following: "I believe catechism is the best apologetics training tool we have at our disposal. Please note that I did not

say 'the best training tool *for children.*' I believe it's the best tool, period."[1] This catechism will give you the knowledge to defend biblical truth, and specifically, why you trust in Jesus Christ as Lord and Savior. By knowing the doctrine taught in the Bible and where it is found in the word, you are able to respond to the world around you by making a clear explanation and defense of the Christian faith. This should also give you confidence and boldness in your witness to those you encounter.

3) Catechizing will help a believer fight and overcome sin. When we rightly know biblical truth, we are better equipped to fight the temptation of sin; we can conform not to the world but to Christ Jesus. Additionally, part of avoiding sin is being able to spot and avoid false teaching. Catechizing will protect us and those around us from being led astray.

I am pleased that it seems there is a modern resurgence in the use of catechisms among many solid Christians. Voddie Baucham again:

This is not a new phenomenon. No doubt, Christians have struggled to find the time and energy to catechize since the advent of catechism. However, I assure you it's worth the effort. There's indeed a great reward that awaits those who will persevere in this matter.[2]

My prayer is that more local churches, and the singles and families within them, will make the time, spend the energy, and experience the reward of using this catechism. May the Lord teach you His truth, using the means He has given, for His glory, your joy, and others' good.

Soli Deo Gloria

Part 1:
Doctrine of God
(Theology Proper)

Word of Truth Catechism

Q1. Who is God?

God is the almighty Creator, Sustainer, and Ruler of everything. He is perfect, and the standard by which all things are measured.

Isaiah 40:28 Have you not known? Have you not heard? The LORD is the everlasting God, the Creator of the ends of the earth. He does not faint or grow weary; his understanding is unsearchable.

Colossians 1:16-17 For by him [Jesus] all things were created, in heaven and on earth, visible and invisible, whether thrones or dominions or rulers or authorities — all things were created through him and for him. And he is before all things, and in him all things hold together.

Matthew 5:48 "You therefore must be perfect, as your heavenly Father is perfect."

1 John 1:5 This is the message we have heard from him and proclaim to you, that God is light, and in him is no darkness at all.

Psalm 5:5 The boastful shall not stand before your eyes; you hate all evildoers.

Q2. Are there more gods than one?

No. There is only one true God.

Deuteronomy 6:4 (NASB) "Hear, O Israel! The LORD is our God, the LORD is one!"

Isaiah 45:22 (NASB) "Turn to Me and be saved, all the ends of the earth; For I am God, and there is no other."

Jeremiah 10:10 (NKJV) But the LORD is the true God; He is the living God and the everlasting King. ...

Deuteronomy 4:35 "To you it was shown, that you might know that the LORD is God; there is no other besides him."

Q3. God exists eternally as how many persons?

God exists eternally as one God, three Persons: God the Father, God the Son (Jesus), and God the Holy Spirit.

2 Corinthians 13:14 (NASB) The grace of the Lord Jesus Christ, and the love of God, and the fellowship of the Holy Spirit, be with you all.

Matthew 3:16-17 And when Jesus was baptized, immediately he went up from the water, and behold, the heavens were opened to him, and he saw the Spirit of God descending like a dove and coming to rest on him; and behold, a voice from heaven said, "This is my beloved Son, with whom I am well pleased."

Matthew 28:19 "Go therefore and make disciples of all the nations, baptizing them in the name of the Father and of the Son and of the Holy Spirit"

John 14:26 (NASB) "But the Helper, the Holy Spirit, whom the Father will send in My name, He will teach you all things, and bring to your remembrance all that I said to you."

Deuteronomy 6:4 (NASB) "Hear, O Israel! The Lord is our God, the Lord is one!"

Trinity: One God, three Persons. There is but one eternal Godhead that exists in three co-equal, co-eternal Persons: God the Father, God the Son, and God the Holy Spirit. Each Person is fully and completely God; each has the same essence and is described in Scripture as possessing the attributes of God.

Q4. Does God have a beginning or an end?

No. God is eternal, self-existent, and self-sufficient. He is not subject to time, and He has no beginning and no end.

Revelation 1:8 "I am the Alpha and the Omega," says the Lord God, "who is and who was and who is to come, the Almighty."

Isaiah 26:4 "Trust in the LORD forever, for the LORD God is an everlasting rock."

Psalm 90:2 Before the mountains were brought forth, or ever you had formed the earth and the world, from everlasting to everlasting you are God.

John 5:26 "For as the Father has life in himself, so he has granted the Son also to have life in himself."

The Aseity of God: God does not owe His existence to anything or anyone outside Himself, nor does He need anything beyond Himself to maintain His existence. He is self-contained, self-existent, self-sufficient, and independent.

Q5. Does God have a body?

God is spirit.
God the Son, Jesus, took on flesh at the incarnation and will have that body forever.

John 4:24 "God is spirit, and those who worship him must worship in spirit and truth."

Colossians 1:15 He is the image of the invisible God, the firstborn of all creation.

Luke 1:31 (NASB) "And behold, you will conceive in your womb and bear a son, and you shall name Him Jesus."

Matthew 1:23 "Behold, the virgin shall conceive and bear a son, and they shall call his name Immanuel" (which means, God with us).

Luke 24:39 (NASB) "See My hands and My feet, that it is I Myself; touch Me and see, for a spirit does not have flesh and bones as you see that I have."

The Spirituality of God: God is spirit. He exists as a being that has no parts or dimensions, is not made of any matter, and is more excellent than any other kind of existence. He is an invisible, immaterial, and infinite being that is fundamentally distinct from visible, material, and finite creatures.

Q6. How can we know about God?

We can never fully understand all of God exhaustively, yet we can know God truly. We can know about God through His creation and His revelation. The holy Bible is the true and final source for our understanding of God and His will for His creation.

Romans 11:33 Oh, the depth of the riches and wisdom and knowledge of God! How unsearchable are his judgments and how inscrutable his ways!

Romans 1:19-20 For what can be known about God is plain to them, because God has shown it to them. For his invisible attributes, namely, his eternal power and divine nature, have been clearly perceived, ever since the creation of the world, in the things that have been made. So they are without excuse.

2 Timothy 3:16-17 All Scripture is breathed out by God and profitable for teaching, for reproof, for correction, and for training in righteousness, that the man of God may be complete, equipped for every good work.

1 John 5:20 And we know that the Son of God has come and has given us understanding, so that we may know him who is true; and we are in him who is true, in his Son Jesus Christ. He is the true God and eternal life.

Jeremiah 9:24 (NKJV) "But let him who glories glory in this, That he understands and knows Me, That I am the LORD, exercising lovingkindness, judgment, and righteousness in the earth. For in these I delight," says the LORD.

Q7. Describe God: What is God like?

He is holy, He is good, He is love, He is wrath, He is just, He is wise, and He is in control of all things.

Revelation 4:8 "Holy, holy, holy, is the Lord God Almighty, who was and is and is to come!"

Psalm 106:1 Praise the LORD. Oh give thanks to the LORD, for he is good; for his steadfast love endures forever!

1 John 4:8 Anyone who does not love does not know God, because God is love.

Hebrews 12:29 for our God is a consuming fire.

Revelation 16:7 ... "Yes, Lord God the Almighty, true and just are your judgments!"

Job 12:13 "With God are wisdom and might; he has counsel and understanding."

Psalm 115:3 Our God is in the heavens; he does all that he pleases.

See the Glossary for some of *God's attributes.*

Q8. What is the glory of God?

The glory of God is His holiness, infinite beauty, and the greatness of His limitless perfection shining out to all of creation.

Isaiah 6:3 And one called to another and said: "Holy, holy, holy is the LORD of hosts; the whole earth is full of his glory!"

Psalm 19:1 The heavens declare the glory of God and the sky above proclaims his handiwork.

Habakkuk 2:14 (NASB) "For the earth will be filled with the knowledge of the glory of the Lord, as the waters cover the sea."

Ezekiel 10:4 And the glory of the LORD went up from the cherub to the threshold of the house, and the house was filled with the cloud, and the court was filled with the brightness of the glory of the LORD.

Q9. Where is God?
God is everywhere. He is omnipresent.

Jeremiah 23:24 "Can a man hide himself in secret places so that I cannot see him? declares the LORD. Do I not fill heaven and earth? declares the LORD."

Psalm 139:7-10 (NASB) Where can I go from Your Spirit? Or where can I flee from Your presence? If I ascend to heaven, You are there; If I make my bed in Sheol, behold, You are there. If I take the wings of the dawn, if I dwell in the remotest part of the sea, even there Your hand will lead me, and Your right hand will lay hold of me.

1 Kings 8:27 (NASB) "But will God indeed dwell on the earth? Behold, heaven and the highest heaven cannot contain You, how much less this house which I have built!"

John 14:23 Jesus answered him, "If anyone loves me, he will keep my word, and my Father will love him, and we will come to him and make our home with him."

Omnipresent (om-nuh-prez-uh nt): God does not have size or spatial dimensions and is present at every point of space with His whole being. Nothing in the universe exists outside the presence of God.

Q10. Can we see God?

No. We cannot see God, but He always sees us. We will see Him when Jesus returns at His second coming to judge the world and to save the redeemed from sin and punishment.

John 1:18 (HCSB) No one has ever seen God. The One and Only Son—the One who is at the Father's side—He has revealed Him.

Colossians 1:15 He [Jesus] is the image of the invisible God, the firstborn of all creation.

1 Timothy 1:17 To the King of the ages, immortal, invisible, the only God, be honor and glory forever and ever. Amen.

Acts 1:11 "... This Jesus, who was taken up from you into heaven, will come in the same way as you saw him go into heaven."

1 Thessalonians 4:16 (NASB) For the Lord Himself will descend from heaven with a shout, with the voice of the archangel and with the trumpet of God, and the dead in Christ will rise first.

Q11. Does God know all things?

Yes. God knows all things eternally. Nothing can be hidden from God. He is omniscient.

1 John 3:20 for whenever our heart condemns us, God is greater than our heart, and he knows everything.

Job 37:16 (NASB) "Do you know about the layers of the thick clouds, the wonders of one perfect in knowledge"

Hebrews 4:12-13 For the word of God is living and active, sharper than any two-edged sword, piercing to the division of soul and of spirit, of joints and of marrow, and discerning the thoughts and intentions of the heart. And no creature is hidden from his sight, but all are naked and exposed to the eyes of him to whom we must give account.

Matthew 10:29 "Are not two sparrows sold for a penny? And not one of them will fall to the ground apart from your Father."

Omniscient (om-nish-uh nt): God has perfect, complete knowledge. He knows all things that exist and all things that could have existed. He never learns, nor does He forget. God cannot grow in understanding, knowledge, or wisdom, because He lacks nothing.

Q12. Is God all-powerful?

Yes. God is able to do all His holy will. He is omnipotent.

Jeremiah 32:27 "Behold, I am the LORD, the God of all flesh. Is anything too hard for me?"

Job 42:2 "I know that you can do all things, and that no purpose of yours can be thwarted."

Matthew 19:26 But Jesus looked at them and said, "With man this is impossible, but with God all things are possible."

Luke 1:37 (NASB) "For nothing will be impossible with God."

Jeremiah 32:17 (NASB) "'Ah Lord GOD! Behold, You have made the heavens and the earth by Your great power and by Your outstretched arm! Nothing is too difficult for You'"

Daniel 4:35 (NASB) "All the inhabitants of the earth are accounted as nothing, but He does according to His will in the host of heaven and among the inhabitants of earth; and no one can ward off His hand or say to Him, 'What have You done?'"

Omnipotent (om-nip-uh-tuh nt): God is able to do all His holy will. He is all-powerful.

Q13. Is God good?

Yes. God is truly, perfectly good.

Psalm 106:1 Praise the LORD. Oh give thanks to the LORD, for he is good; for his steadfast love endures forever!

Psalm 31:19 (NASB) How great is Your goodness, which You have stored up for those who fear You, which You have wrought for those who take refuge in You, before the sons of men!

James 1:13 Let no one say when he is tempted, "I am being tempted by God," for God cannot be tempted with evil, and he himself tempts no one.

Acts 14:17 (NASB) "... [God] did not leave Himself without witness, in that He did good and gave you rains from heaven and fruitful seasons, satisfying your hearts with food and gladness."

The Goodness of God: All that God is and does is perfectly good, and He alone is the final standard of good. There is such an absolute perfection in God's nature and being that nothing is lacking or defective in Him, and nothing can be added to make Him better.

Q14. Who made each of us and every other created thing?

God made us and every other created thing.

Genesis 1:1 In the beginning, God created the heavens and the earth.

John 1:3 All things were made through him, and without him was not any thing made that was made.

Genesis 1:27 So God created man in his own image, in the image of God he created him; male and female he created them.

Colossians 1:16 For by him all things were created, in heaven and on earth, visible and invisible, whether thrones or dominions or rulers or authorities — all things were created through him and for him.

Q15. Why did God make us?
God made us to glorify Him, so His glory would be known and praised.

Isaiah 43:7 "everyone who is called by my name, whom I created for my glory, whom I formed and made."

1 Corinthians 10:31 (NASB) Whether, then, you eat or drink or whatever you do, do all to the glory of God.

Isaiah 48:11 "For my own sake, for my own sake, I do it, for how should my name be profaned? My glory I will not give to another."

Psalm 96:1-3 (NASB) Sing to the LORD a new song; Sing to the LORD, all the earth. Sing to the LORD, bless His name; Proclaim good tidings of His salvation from day to day. Tell of His glory among the nations, His wonderful deeds among all the peoples.

Q16. How should we glorify God?

We glorify God by trusting in Jesus, enjoying Him, treasuring Him, growing in our knowledge of Him, believing His words, obeying His commands, and by showing and telling the world how great He is.

Hebrews 11:6 (NASB) And without faith it is impossible to please Him ...

Deuteronomy 11:1 "You shall therefore love the LORD your God and keep his charge, his statutes, his rules, and his commandments always."

Ecclesiastes 12:13 The end of the matter; all has been heard. Fear God and keep his commandments, for this is the whole duty of man.

1 Corinthians 10:31 (NASB) Whether, then, you eat or drink or whatever you do, do all to the glory of God.

Jeremiah 9:24 (NKJV) "But let him who glories glory in this, That he understands and knows Me, That I am the LORD, exercising lovingkindness, judgment, and righteousness in the earth. For in these I delight," says the LORD.

Q17. What does it mean to fear God?

For the saved, fearing God is not a fear of His wrath; rather, it is an awe — a reverence — for the holiness and majesty of God. It is also a humbleness and reasonable trembling towards God's seriousness and power.

Proverbs 1:7 (NASB) The fear of the LORD is the beginning of knowledge; fools despise wisdom and instruction.

2 Corinthians 7:1 Since we have these promises, beloved, let us cleanse ourselves from every defilement of body and spirit, bringing holiness to completion in the fear of God.

Ecclesiastes 12:13 The end of the matter; all has been heard. Fear God and keep his commandments, for this is the whole duty of man.

Matthew 10:28 "And do not fear those who kill the body but cannot kill the soul. Rather fear him who can destroy both soul and body in hell."

1 Peter 1:17 And if you call on him as Father who judges impartially according to each one's deeds, conduct yourselves with fear throughout the time of your exile

Q18. Does God control and have authority over all things?

Yes. He rules in and over all things. He is in control of all things. God does all that He wills with creation.

Psalm 115:3 Our God is in the heavens; he does all that he pleases.

Ephesians 1:11 In him we have obtained an inheritance, having been predestined according to the purpose of him who works all things according to the counsel of his will

Daniel 4:35 (NASB) "All the inhabitants of the earth are accounted as nothing, but He does according to His will in the host of heaven and among the inhabitants of earth; and no one can ward off His hand or say to Him, 'What have You done?'"

Isaiah 45:7 "I form light and create darkness, I make well-being and create calamity, I am the LORD, who does all these things."

Isaiah 46:10 "declaring the end from the beginning and from ancient times things not yet done, saying, 'My counsel shall stand, and I will accomplish all my purpose'"

God's Sovereignty: As the one true Ruler and Owner of creation, God has rightful and complete authority over all things. He has legitimate claim to absolute lordship, and His governing is just.

God's Providence: God controls and directs all things, and He does so to fulfill His purposes after the counsel of His own holy will for His glory. God is the Supreme Being who answers to no one and who has the absolute right to do with His creation as He desires; nothing happens without His ordination.

For further study on God's sovereignty and providence, see the following: **Nature, Weather** (Psalm 104:14; Matthew 5:45); **Things that seem random to us** (Proverbs 16:33); **Governments & Rulers** (Romans 13:1; Job 12:23); **All aspects of human lives** (Psalm 139:16; Psalm 139:13; Proverbs 16:9; Jeremiah 10:23); **In saving whomever is saved** (Ephesians 1:4-5; Romans 9:15-16)

Q19. What are angels?

Angels are created spiritual beings who have limited power and are under God's control.

Genesis 1:31 And God saw everything that he had made, and behold, it was very good. And there was evening and there was morning, the sixth day.

Nehemiah 9:6 "You are the LORD, you alone. You have made heaven, the heaven of heavens, with all their host, the earth and all that is on it, the seas and all that is in them; and you preserve all of them; and the host of heaven worships you."

Hebrews 2:7-8 "You made him [Jesus] for a little while lower than the angels; you have crowned him with glory and honor, putting everything in subjection under his feet."

Hebrews 1:14 Are they [elect angels] not all ministering spirits sent out to serve for the sake of those who are to inherit salvation?

1 Corinthians 6:3 Do you not know that we are to judge angels? ...

Q20. What kinds of angels are there?

The Bible tells us of two kinds of angels: elect angels and fallen angels (demons).
Elect angels are those whom God ordained not to fall but to serve and enjoy God and His ways. Fallen angels (demons) are evil angels who sinned against God and now continually work evil in creation. There is no redemption for fallen angels.

Psalm 103:20 Bless the LORD, O you his angels, you mighty ones who do his word, obeying the voice of his word!

Jude 1:6 And the angels who did not stay within their own position of authority, but left their proper dwelling, he has kept in eternal chains under gloomy darkness until the judgment of the great day

1 Timothy 5:21 In the presence of God and of Christ Jesus and of the elect angels I charge you to keep these rules without prejudging, doing nothing from partiality.

1 Timothy 4:1 Now the Spirit expressly says that in later times some will depart from the faith by devoting themselves to deceitful spirits and teachings of demons

James 2:19 You believe that God is one; you do well. Even the demons believe — and shudder!

Q21. Who is Satan?

Satan opposes God as the chief of all fallen angels by deceiving, tempting, and lying. Satan only has the access and ability that God permits him.

1 John 3:8 Whoever makes a practice of sinning is of the devil, for the devil has been sinning from the beginning. The reason the Son of God appeared was to destroy the works of the devil.

1 Peter 5:8 Be sober-minded; be watchful. Your adversary the devil prowls around like a roaring lion, seeking someone to devour.

John 8:44 (NASB) "You are of your father the devil, and you want to do the desires of your father. He was a murderer from the beginning, and does not stand in the truth because there is no truth in him. Whenever he speaks a lie, he speaks from his own nature, for he is a liar and the father of lies."

James 4:7 Submit yourselves therefore to God. Resist the devil, and he will flee from you.

Revelation 12:10 (NASB) Then I heard a loud voice in heaven, saying, "Now the salvation, and the power, and the kingdom of our God and the authority of His Christ have come, for the accuser of our brethren has been thrown down, he who accuses them before our God day and night."

Genesis 3:15 "I will put enmity between you and the woman, and between your offspring and her offspring; he shall bruise your head, and you shall bruise his heel."

More names in Scripture for Satan: the devil, the enemy, the tempter, the father of lies, the adversary, and the accuser.

Part 2:
Doctrine of the
Word of God
(Bibliology)

Q22. What is the Bible?

The Bible is God's inspired, infallible, inerrant, authoritative, written word.

2 Timothy 3:16-17 All Scripture is breathed out by God and profitable for teaching, for reproof, for correction, and for training in righteousness, that the man of God may be complete, equipped for every good work.

2 Peter 1:20-21 knowing this first of all, that no prophecy of Scripture comes from someone's own interpretation. For no prophecy was ever produced by the will of man, but men spoke from God as they were carried along by the Holy Spirit.

Deuteronomy 18:20-22 (NASB) "'But the prophet who speaks a word presumptuously in My name which I have not commanded him to speak, or which he speaks in the name of other gods, that prophet shall die.' You may say in your heart, 'How will we know the word which the LORD has not spoken?' When a prophet speaks in the name of the LORD, if the thing does not come about or come true, that is the thing which the LORD has not spoken. The prophet has spoken it presumptuously; you shall not be afraid of him."

Psalm 119:4 You have commanded your precepts to be kept diligently.

Necessity of Scripture: We need the Bible; we cannot rightly know God or what He requires of man without the special revelation of the Bible.

Sufficiency of Scripture: The Bible is enough; it tells us who God is, who man is in relation to Him, what God has done, and what God requires of man.

Authority of Scripture: As God's word, the Bible is our rule; it is always the final and authoritative word.

Q23. Who wrote the Bible?

The Bible was written by chosen men who were taught and carried along by the Holy Spirit.

2 Peter 1:20-21 knowing this first of all, that no prophecy of Scripture comes from someone's own interpretation. For no prophecy was ever produced by the will of man, but men spoke from God as they were carried along by the Holy Spirit.

2 Timothy 3:16-17 All Scripture is breathed out by God and profitable for teaching, for reproof, for correction, and for training in righteousness, that the man of God may be complete, equipped for every good work.

Haggai 1:7 "Thus says the LORD of hosts: Consider your ways."

2 Peter 3:1-2 (NASB) This is now, beloved, the second letter I am writing to you in which I am stirring up your sincere mind by way of reminder, that you should remember the words spoken beforehand by the holy prophets and the commandment of the Lord and Savior spoken by your apostles.

Q24. Can we trust the Bible?

Yes. The Bible is completely true and without error in its original manuscripts.

2 Peter 1:20-21 knowing this first of all, that no prophecy of Scripture comes from someone's own interpretation. For no prophecy was ever produced by the will of man, but men spoke from God as they were carried along by the Holy Spirit.

Romans 15:4 (NASB) For whatever was written in earlier times was written for our instruction, so that through perseverance and the encouragement of the Scriptures we might have hope.

Psalm 12:6 The words of the LORD are pure words, like silver refined in a furnace on the ground, purified seven times.

Psalm 19:7 The law of the LORD is perfect, reviving the soul; the testimony of the LORD is sure, making wise the simple

Luke 24:27 And beginning with Moses and all the Prophets, he [Jesus] interpreted to them in all the Scriptures the things concerning himself.

Inerrancy of Scripture (Inerrant): The Bible, in the original manuscripts, is without error in all its teaching; it does not affirm anything that is contrary to fact. The Bible is a reflection of its perfect Author.

Infallibility of Scripture (Infallible): The Bible never fails. It is completely trustworthy as the sole objective source of all God has given us about Himself, His plan for humanity, and the life of faith. The Bible will not fail to accomplish its purpose.

Q25. What is the Bible *primarily* about?

The Bible is primarily about God: who He is and how He works. It tells us of His work in creation and the redemption of His chosen people within fallen man.

Luke 24:27 And beginning with Moses and all the Prophets, he [Jesus] interpreted to them in all the Scriptures the things concerning himself.

John 5:39 You search the Scriptures because you think that in them you have eternal life; and it is they that bear witness about me

Deuteronomy 29:29 "The secret things belong to the LORD our God, but the things that are revealed belong to us and to our children forever, that we may do all the words of this law."

Jeremiah 9:24 (NKJV) "But let him who glories glory in this, That he understands and knows Me, That I am the LORD, exercising lovingkindness, judgment, and righteousness in the earth. For in these I delight," says the LORD.

Mark 13:31 "Heaven and earth will pass away, but my words will not pass away."

Q26. How is the Bible to be read and heard?

The Bible is to be read and heard with joy, diligence, respect, carefulness, and prayer, that we may accept sound doctrine with faith, store it in our hearts, and practice it in our lives. In it we find God's revealed will; therefore, we study it to know, trust, love, and obey God.

Psalm 119:11 I have stored up your word in my heart, that I might not sin against you.

1 Peter 3:15 but in your hearts honor Christ the Lord as holy, always being prepared to make a defense to anyone who asks you for a reason for the hope that is in you; yet do it with gentleness and respect

Psalm 119:104-105 Through your precepts I get understanding; therefore I hate every false way. Your word is a lamp to my feet and a light to my path.

2 Timothy 3:16-17 All Scripture is breathed out by God and profitable for teaching, for reproof, for correction, and for training in righteousness, that the man of God may be complete, equipped for every good work.

Psalm 1:1-2 Blessed is the man who walks not in the counsel of the wicked, nor stands in the way of sinners, nor sits in the seat of scoffers; but his delight is in the law of the LORD, and on his law he meditates day and night.

Part 3:
Doctrine of Man
(Anthropology)

Q27. How did God create the first man and woman?

God formed Adam from the dust of the ground and then formed Eve from the rib of Adam.

Genesis 2:7 then the LORD God formed the man of dust from the ground and breathed into his nostrils the breath of life, and the man became a living creature.

Genesis 2:22-23 And the rib that the LORD God had taken from the man he made into a woman and brought her to the man. Then the man said, "This at last is bone of my bones and flesh of my flesh; she shall be called Woman, because she was taken out of Man."

Genesis 1:26-27 Then God said, "Let us make man in our image, after our likeness. And let them have dominion over the fish of the sea and over the birds of the heavens and over the livestock and over all the earth and over every creeping thing that creeps on the earth." So God created man in his own image, in the image of God he created him; male and female he created them.

Q28. In what condition did God create Adam and Eve?

They were created good, blessed, and with no sin.

Genesis 1:26-27 Then God said, "Let us make man in our image, after our likeness. And let them have dominion over the fish of the sea and over the birds of the heavens and over the livestock and over all the earth and over every creeping thing that creeps on the earth." So God created man in his own image, in the image of God he created him; male and female he created them.

Genesis 1:31 And God saw everything that he had made, and behold, it was very good. And there was evening and there was morning, the sixth day.

Ecclesiastes 7:29 See, this alone I found, that God made man upright, but they have sought out many schemes.

Romans 5:12 (NASB) Therefore, just as through one man sin entered into the world, and death through sin, and so death spread to all men, because all sinned

Q29. What is marriage?

Marriage is a covenant relationship whereby God joins together one man and one woman into a one-flesh union designed to be faithful and last until the couple is separated by death.

Genesis 1:27-28 So God created man in his own image, in the image of God he created him; male and female he created them. And God blessed them. And God said to them, "Be fruitful and multiply and fill the earth and subdue it ..."

Mark 10:6-9 "But from the beginning of creation, 'God made them male and female.' Therefore a man shall leave his father and mother and hold fast to his wife, and the two shall become one flesh.' So they are no longer two but one flesh. What therefore God has joined together, let not man separate."

Ephesians 5:32 This mystery is profound, and I am saying that it refers to Christ and the church.

Romans 7:2-3 For a married woman is bound by law to her husband while he lives, but if her husband dies she is released from the law of marriage. Accordingly, she will be called an adulteress if she lives with another man while her husband is alive. But if her husband dies, she is free from that law, and if she marries another man she is not an adulteress.

Q30. What roles did God ordain for men and women within the family?

God has ordained the role of the husband to lovingly lead his wife and family. God has ordained the role of the wife to joyfully submit to her husband's leadership as his helper.

Ephesians 5:22-33 Wives, submit to your own husbands, as to the Lord. For the husband is the head of the wife even as Christ is the head of the church, his body, and is himself its Savior. Now as the church submits to Christ, so also wives should submit in everything to their husbands. Husbands, love your wives, as Christ loved the church and gave himself up for her by the washing of water with the word, so that he might present the church to himself in splendor, without spot or wrinkle or any such thing, that she might be holy and without blemish. In the same way husbands should love their wives as their own bodies. He who loves his wife loves himself. For no one ever hated his own flesh, but nourishes and cherishes it, just as Christ does the church, because we are members of his body. "Therefore a man shall leave his father and mother and hold fast to his wife, and the two shall become one flesh." This mystery is profound, and I am saying that it refers to Christ and the church. However, let each one of you love his wife as himself, and let the wife see that she respects her husband.

Genesis 2:18 Then the LORD God said, "It is not good that the man should be alone; I will make him a helper fit for him."

Titus 2:5 [Wives are] to be self-controlled, pure, working at home, kind, and submissive to their own husbands, that the word of God may not be reviled.

1 Timothy 3:4 He must manage his own household well, with all dignity keeping his children submissive

Q31. Is man or woman more important than the other?

No. Men and women are equal in dignity and value; both are created in the image of God.

Genesis 1:26-27 Then God said, "Let us make man in our image, after our likeness. And let them have dominion over the fish of the sea and over the birds of the heavens and over the livestock and over all the earth and over every creeping thing that creeps on the earth." So God created man in his own image, in the image of God he created him; male and female he created them.

Galatians 5:14 For the whole law is fulfilled in one word: "You shall love your neighbor as yourself."

Galatians 3:28 There is neither Jew nor Greek, there is neither slave nor free, there is no male and female, for you are all one in Christ Jesus.

Romans 3:23 for all have sinned and fall short of the glory of God

Q32. Should everyone get married?

No. God has blessed some with the gift of singleness and some with the gift of marriage. Both singleness and marriage are valued by God and accomplish His purposes.

1 Corinthians 7:7-9 I wish that all were as I myself am. But each has his own gift from God, one of one kind and one of another. To the unmarried and the widows I say that it is good for them to remain single as I am. But if they cannot exercise self-control, they should marry. For it is better to marry than to burn with passion.

1 Corinthians 7:25-27 Now concerning the betrothed, I have no command from the Lord, but I give my judgment as one who by the Lord's mercy is trustworthy. I think that in view of the present distress it is good for a person to remain as he is. Are you bound to a wife? Do not seek to be free. Are you free from a wife? Do not seek a wife.

Matthew 19:12 "For there are eunuchs who have been so from birth, and there are eunuchs who have been made eunuchs by men, and there are eunuchs who have made themselves eunuchs for the sake of the kingdom of heaven. Let the one who is able to receive this receive it."

Philippians 4:11 Not that I am speaking of being in need, for I have learned in whatever situation I am to be content.

Part 4:
Doctrine of Sin
(Hamartiology)

Q33. What is sin?

Sin is disobeying God; sin is any disobedience in heart or deed to God's perfect law and commands.

1 John 3:4 Everyone who makes a practice of sinning also practices lawlessness; sin is lawlessness.

James 2:10 For whoever keeps the whole law and yet stumbles at just one point is guilty of breaking all of it.

Romans 3:10-12 as it is written: "None is righteous, no, not one; no one understands; no one seeks for God. All have turned aside; together they have become worthless; no one does good, not even one."

Luke 16:15 And he said to them, "You are those who justify yourselves before men, but God knows your hearts. For what is exalted among men is an abomination in the sight of God."

Genesis 6:5 The LORD saw that the wickedness of man was great in the earth, and that every intention of the thoughts of his heart was only evil continually

Romans 3:23 for all have sinned and fall short of the glory of God

Disobedience in Heart: Having the wrong state of mind, motivation, or desire behind what we do or feel.

Disobedience in Deed: Doing or saying what God forbids, or not doing or saying what God commands.

Q34. What is the sin of idolatry?

Idolatry is worshiping or finding hope, identity, significance, purpose, or security in anything other than in God, our Creator.

Colossians 3:5 Put to death therefore what is earthly in you: sexual immorality, impurity, passion, evil desire, and covetousness, which is idolatry.

Romans 1:25 because they exchanged the truth about God for a lie and worshiped and served the creature rather than the Creator, who is blessed forever! Amen.

Jonah 2:8 Those who pay regard to vain idols forsake their hope of steadfast love.

Exodus 20:3 "You shall have no other gods before me."

1 Corinthians 10:14 Therefore, my beloved, flee from idolatry.

Q35. How did Adam and Eve sin?

Satan tempted and deceived Eve to disobey God by eating the forbidden fruit, then she gave it to Adam, and he also disobeyed God. Adam and Eve did not fully trust God's word, so they were vulnerable to temptation.

Genesis 2:16-17 And the LORD God commanded the man, saying, "You may surely eat of every tree of the garden, but of the tree of the knowledge of good and evil you shall not eat, for in the day that you eat of it you shall surely die."

Genesis 3:1 Now the serpent was more crafty than any other beast of the field that the LORD God had made. He said to the woman, "Did God actually say, 'You shall not eat of any tree in the garden'?"

Genesis 3:6 ... she took of its fruit and ate, and she also gave some to her husband who was with her, and he ate.

Genesis 3:13 Then the LORD God said to the woman, "What is this that you have done?" The woman said, "The serpent deceived me, and I ate."

Q36. Why does Adam's sin affect everyone else?

God chose Adam to act as the representative of the entire human race. With the test that God set before Adam, He was testing the whole of mankind. In this, Adam accurately represented us.

Romans 5:12 (NASB) Therefore, just as through one man sin entered into the world, and death through sin, and so death spread to all men, because all sinned

1 Corinthians 15:21-22 For as by a man came death, by a man has come also the resurrection of the dead. For as in Adam all die ...

Romans 1:21 For although they knew God, they did not honor him as God or give thanks to him, but they became futile in their thinking, and their foolish hearts were darkened.

Romans 3:10-12 as it is written: "None is righteous, no, not one; no one understands; no one seeks for God. All have turned aside; together they have become worthless; no one does good, not even one."

Federal Headship of Adam: God chose Adam as the Federal Head (representative) of all mankind. Because Adam failed to obey God's commands perfectly, all those he represented receive the results of his disobedience. Given God's perfect wisdom, we can never argue that Adam was a poor choice to represent us. God's choice of Adam as the first Federal Head was an infallible (perfect) choice; Adam represented us accurately. If we are to be reconciled to God, we need a second and final Federal Head to redeem and represent us. For the salvation of the elect, God ordained Jesus as the second and final Federal Head.

Q37. What happened to mankind because of sin?

After the sin of Adam, all people are guilty: born sinful by nature, enslaved to sin, and practice sin willingly and continually; therefore, all are due the just penalty of God's perfect wrath.

Psalm 51:5 Behold, I was brought forth in iniquity, and in sin did my mother conceive me.

Romans 5:12 (NASB) Therefore, just as through one man sin entered into the world, and death through sin, and so death spread to all men, because all sinned

Genesis 6:5 The LORD saw that the wickedness of man was great in the earth, and that every intention of the thoughts of his heart was only evil continually.

Romans 6:23 For the wages of sin is death ...

Matthew 25:46 (NASB) "These [all unbelievers] will go away into eternal punishment ..."

Original Sin: The inherited guilt and corruption of man's nature as a direct result of Adam's sin. Because of God's system of headship, when Adam sinned, in some sense, all of mankind sinned with him; therefore, Adam's guilt is every person's guilt. In addition to the legal guilt that God imputes to each person, everyone also inherits a sinful nature and the other consequences brought on because of Adam's sin.

(Also see Glossary terms: *Total Depravity* and *Human Inability*)

Q38. What happened to the rest of creation because of sin?

Creation is cursed and broken because of sin. It does not function in the "good" way in which God created it.

Genesis 3:17-18 (NIV1984) ... "Cursed is the ground because of you; through painful toil you will eat of it all the days of your life. It will produce thorns and thistles for you, and you will eat the plants of the field."

Romans 8:20 For the creation was subjected to futility, not willingly, but because of him who subjected it ...

Luke 21:11 "There will be great earthquakes, and in various places famines and pestilences. And there will be terrors and great signs from heaven."

Deuteronomy 11:17 "then the anger of the LORD will be kindled against you, and he will shut up the heavens, so that there will be no rain, and the land will yield no fruit, and you will perish quickly off the good land that the LORD is giving you."

Job 12:15 "If he withholds the waters, they dry up; if he sends them out, they overwhelm the land."

Part 5:
Commands
(Law)

Q39. Biblically, what is law?

Law is the requirements on man often expressed through commands that God has given.

Psalm 19:7 The law of the LORD is perfect, reviving the soul; the testimony of the LORD is sure, making wise the simple

Psalm 119:97 Oh how I love your law! It is my meditation all the day.

John 14:15 (NKJV) "If you love Me, keep My commandments."

Deuteronomy 10:4 And [God] wrote on the tablets, in the same writing as before, the Ten Commandments that the LORD had spoken to you on the mountain out of the midst of the fire on the day of the assembly. And the LORD gave them to me.

Romans 2:15-16 [Gentiles] show that the work of the law is written on their hearts, while their conscience also bears witness, and their conflicting thoughts accuse or even excuse them on that day when, according to my gospel, God judges the secrets of men by Christ Jesus.

Universal Moral Law (Natural Law): Unchanging law and commands based on the right and character of God, to which man is held accountable for all of life. Universal Moral Law is written in the hearts of all people, leaving them without excuse in disobedience.

Positive Law: Law and commands based on the will of God for a particular people, a particular purpose, and a particular time.

Q40. Who can perfectly obey God's law?

Because of sin, fallen man cannot rightly obey God's law. Only Christ Jesus obeyed God's law perfectly and did not sin.

Romans 3:23 for all have sinned and fall short of the glory of God

Romans 3:20 For by works of the law no human being will be justified in his sight, since through the law comes knowledge of sin.

Hebrews 4:15 (NIV1984) For we do not have a high priest who is unable to sympathize with our weaknesses, but we have one who has been tempted in every way, just as we are — yet was without sin.

Q41. If fallen man cannot perfectly obey God's law, why did God give it?

God's law displays His perfections and glory, informs mankind what is required of us, and reveals our sin and our desperate need for Jesus.

John 5:39 You search the Scriptures because you think that in them you have eternal life; and it is they that bear witness about me

Romans 3:20 (NIV1984) Therefore no one will be declared righteous in his sight by observing the law; rather, through the law we become conscious of sin.

Galatians 3:11 Now it is evident that no one is justified before God by the law, for "The righteous shall live by faith."

Romans 3:31 Do we then overthrow the law by this faith? By no means! On the contrary, we uphold the law.

Romans 7:22 For I delight in the law of God, in my inner being

Romans 2:14-16 For when Gentiles, who do not have the law, by nature do what the law requires, they are a law to themselves, even though they do not have the law. They show that the work of the law is written on their hearts, while their conscience also bears witness, and their conflicting thoughts accuse or even excuse them on that day when, according to my gospel, God judges the secrets of men by Christ Jesus.

Threefold Use of the Universal Moral Law:

First Function: It reveals both the perfect righteousness of God and man's own sinfulness and shortcomings.

Second Function: It aids in restraining evil throughout mankind. To some degree, it secures civil order and keeps mankind from practicing even more sin than what is done.

Third Function: It informs the saved of the good works that God has planned for them; it aids them to learn in truth with greater confidence what the will of the Lord is.

Q42. What are the greatest commandments?

First, to love God. And second, to love our neighbor.

Matthew 22:37-40 And he said to him, "You shall love the Lord your God with all your heart and with all your soul and with all your mind. This is the great and first commandment. And a second is like it: You shall love your neighbor as yourself. On these two commandments depend all the Law and the Prophets."

1 John 4:21 And this commandment we have from him: whoever loves God must also love his brother.

1 John 4:8 Anyone who does not love does not know God, because God is love.

Q43. How should we love God?

We love God with all our heart and with all our soul and with all our mind. We do this by trusting in Jesus, enjoying Him, treasuring Him, growing in our knowledge of Him, believing His words, obeying His commands, and showing and telling the world how great He is.

John 6:29 Jesus answered them, "This is the work of God, that you believe in him [Jesus] whom he has sent."

John 15:11 "These things I [Jesus] have spoken to you, that my joy may be in you, and that your joy may be full."

John 14:15 [Jesus said] "If you love me, you will keep my commandments."

Colossians 1:10 so as to walk in a manner worthy of the Lord, fully pleasing to him, bearing fruit in every good work and increasing in the knowledge of God

Matthew 28:19-20 "Go therefore and make disciples of all nations, baptizing them in the name of the Father and of the Son and of the Holy Spirit, teaching them to observe all that I have commanded you. ..."

Q44. How should we love our neighbor?

We should love our neighbor as ourselves, treating each one how we want to be treated. True love for our neighbor is sacrificial, truthful, and selfless.

Leviticus 19:17-18 "You shall not hate your brother in your heart, but you shall reason frankly with your neighbor, lest you incur sin because of him. You shall not take vengeance or bear a grudge against the sons of your own people, but you shall love your neighbor as yourself: I am the LORD."

Matthew 7:12 So whatever you wish that others would do to you, do also to them ...

Exodus 20:16 "You shall not bear false witness against your neighbor."

John 15:12-13 "This is my commandment, that you love one another [other believers] as I have loved you. Greater love has no one than this, that someone lay down his life for his friends."

1 Corinthians 13:4-7 Love is patient and kind; love does not envy or boast; it is not arrogant or rude. It does not insist on its own way; it is not irritable or resentful; it does not rejoice at wrongdoing, but rejoices with the truth. Love bears all things, believes all things, hopes all things, endures all things.

Romans 12:9 Let love be genuine. Abhor what is evil; hold fast to what is good.

Q45. Why does God give the first commandment: You shall have no other gods before me?

So we will worship only God. He is the one true God.

Exodus 20:3 "You shall have no other gods before me."

Isaiah 42:8 I am the LORD; that is my name; my glory I give to no other, nor my praise to carved idols.

Acts 17:24 The God who made the world and everything in it, being Lord of heaven and earth, does not live in temples made by man

1 Timothy 1:17 To the King of the ages, immortal, invisible, the only God, be honor and glory forever and ever. Amen.

Q46. Why does God give the second commandment: You shall not make for yourself an idol?

So we will serve, worship, and glorify God and nothing else.

Exodus 20:4-5 "You shall not make for yourself a carved image, or any likeness of anything that is in heaven above, or that is in the earth beneath, or that is in the water under the earth. You shall not bow down to them or serve them, for I the LORD your God am a jealous God ..."

Jeremiah 16:20 (NIV1984) "Do people make their own gods? Yes, but they are not gods!"

Isaiah 42:8 I am the LORD; that is my name; my glory I give to no other, nor my praise to carved idols.

1 Samuel 12:21 (NIV1984) "Do not turn away after useless idols. They can do you no good, nor can they rescue you, because they are useless."

Q47. Why does God give the third commandment: You shall not misuse the name of the LORD your God?

So we will respect and honor God as the worthy and holy One.

Exodus 20:7 "You shall not take the name of the LORD your God in vain, for the LORD will not hold him guiltless who takes his name in vain."

Psalm 29:2 Ascribe to the LORD the glory due his name; worship the LORD in the splendor of his holiness.

Psalm 139:19-20 Oh that you would slay the wicked, O God! O men of blood, depart from me! They speak against you with malicious intent; your enemies take your name in vain.

Revelation 15:4 "Who will not fear, O Lord, and glorify your name? For you alone are holy. All nations will come and worship you, for your righteous acts have been revealed."

Q48. Why does God give the fourth commandment: Remember the Sabbath day, to keep it holy?

So we will worship and rest in God and remember the finished work of Jesus.

Exodus 20:8 "Remember the Sabbath day, to keep it holy."

Genesis 2:3 So God blessed the seventh day and made it holy, because on it God rested from all his work that he had done in creation.

Mark 2:27 And he said to them, "The Sabbath was made for man, not man for the Sabbath."

2 Corinthians 1:20 (NIV1984) For no matter how many promises God has made, they are "Yes" in Christ. And so through him the "Amen" is spoken by us to the glory of God.

Hebrews 4:9-10 So then, there remains a Sabbath rest for the people of God, for whoever has entered God's rest has also rested from his works as God did from his.

Q49. Why does God give the fifth commandment: Honor your father and mother?

So we will learn righteous submission by practicing obedience to our parents: honoring their God-given authority in attitude, word, and action. This pleases the Lord.

Exodus 20:12 "Honor your father and your mother ..."

Colossians 3:20 Children, obey your parents in everything, for this pleases the Lord.

Proverbs 6:20-21 My son, keep your father's commandment, and forsake not your mother's teaching. Bind them on your heart always; tie them around your neck.

Proverbs 20:20 If one curses his father or his mother, his lamp will be put out in utter darkness.

Ephesians 6:1 Children, obey your parents in the Lord, for this is right.

Q50. Why does God give the sixth commandment: You shall not murder?

So we will love others, not having sinful hate or anger towards them.

Exodus 20:13 "You shall not murder."

1 John 3:15 Everyone who hates his brother is a murderer, and you know that no murderer has eternal life abiding in him.

Matthew 5:21-22 "You have heard that it was said to those of old, 'You shall not murder; and whoever murders will be liable to judgment.' But I say to you that everyone who is angry with his brother will be liable to judgment ..."

Genesis 1:26 Then God said, "Let us make man in our image, after our likeness. And let them have dominion over the fish of the sea and over the birds of the heavens and over the livestock and over all the earth and over every creeping thing that creeps on the earth."

Q51. Why does God give the seventh commandment: You shall not commit adultery?

So we will love others from a faithful and pure heart.

Exodus 20:14 "You shall not commit adultery."

Matthew 5:8 "Blessed are the pure in heart, for they shall see God."

1 Thessalonians 4:3-5 (NIV1984) It is God's will that you should be sanctified: that you should avoid sexual immorality; that each of you should learn to control his own body in a way that is holy and honorable, not in passionate lust like the heathen, who do not know God

Ephesians 5:3 (NIV1984) But among you there must not be even a hint of sexual immorality, or of any kind of impurity, or of greed, because these are improper for God's holy people.

Q52. Why does God give the eighth commandment: You shall not steal?

So we will be content with what we have and seek to be generous.

Exodus 20:15 "You shall not steal."

Ephesians 4:28 (NIV1984) He who has been stealing must steal no longer, but must work, doing something useful with his own hands, that he may have something to share with those in need.

Hebrews 13:5 Keep your life free from love of money, and be content with what you have, for he has said, "I will never leave you nor forsake you."

Acts 20:35 "... remember the words of the Lord Jesus, how he himself said, 'It is more blessed to give than to receive.'"

Q53. Why does God give the ninth commandment: You shall not give false testimony against your neighbor?

So we will always tell the truth and not speak evil of others.

Exodus 20:16 "You shall not bear false witness against your neighbor."

1 Corinthians 13:6 (NIV1984) Love does not delight in evil but rejoices with the truth.

Leviticus 19:11 (NIV1984) "'... Do not lie. Do not deceive one another.'"

Zechariah 8:16 (NIV1984) "These are the things you are to do: Speak the truth to each other, and render true and sound judgment in your courts"

Q54. Why does God give the tenth commandment: You shall not covet?

So we will be content and satisfied with what God has provided, trusting in His plan.

Exodus 20:17 "You shall not covet your neighbor's house; you shall not covet your neighbor's wife, or his male servant, or his female servant, or his ox, or his donkey, or anything that is your neighbor's."

Philippians 4:11 Not that I am speaking of being in need, for I have learned in whatever situation I am to be content.

Hebrews 13:5 (NIV1984) Keep your lives free from the love of money and be content with what you have, because God has said, "Never will I leave you; never will I forsake you."

Matthew 6:8 "... your [heavenly] Father knows what you need before you ask him."

Part 6:
Divine Covenants
(Covenant Theology)

Word of Truth Catechism

Q55. What is a divine covenant?

A divine covenant is a relational agreement initiated by God that may include obligations, rewards, and/or punishments from Him.

Examples of divine covenants God made with man:

Adamic: Genesis 1:26-30; Genesis 2:16-17; Romans 5:12-21

Noahic: Genesis 9:8-17

Abrahamic: Genesis 12:1-3; 15:18–21; 17:1-14; 22:16-18

Mosaic/Sinaitic: Exodus 19-24

Davidic: 2 Samuel 7:4–16

New Covenant: Jeremiah 31:31-34; Luke 22:19-20; Hebrews 9:15

Q56. What is the Covenant of Redemption?

The Covenant of Redemption is the plan and decree made before creation between God the Father, God the Son, and God the Holy Spirit to graciously redeem the chosen ones from sin and punishment based on the work required of Jesus. All of creation is set in the context of this divine plan.

Ephesians 1:3-11 Blessed be the God and Father of our Lord Jesus Christ, who has blessed us in Christ with every spiritual blessing in the heavenly places, even as he chose us in him before the foundation of the world, that we should be holy and blameless before him. In love he predestined us for adoption as sons through Jesus Christ, according to the purpose of his will, to the praise of his glorious grace, with which he has blessed us in the Beloved. In him we have redemption through his blood, the forgiveness of our trespasses, according to the riches of his grace, which he lavished upon us, in all wisdom and insight making known to us the mystery of his will, according to his purpose, which he set forth in Christ as a plan for the fullness of time, to unite all things in him, things in heaven and things on earth. In him we have obtained an inheritance, having been predestined according to the purpose of him who works all things according to the counsel of his will

2 Timothy 1:8-10 (NASB) Therefore do not be ashamed of the testimony of our Lord or of me His prisoner, but join with me in suffering for the gospel according to the power of God, who has saved us and called us with a holy calling, not according to our works, but according to His own purpose and grace which was granted us in Christ Jesus from all eternity, but now has been revealed by the appearing of our Savior Christ Jesus, who abolished death and brought life and immortality to light through the gospel

(Further study: John 17:1-5; Acts 4:27-28; Isaiah 53:10; John 6:37-39)

Q57. What is the covenant that God made with Adam as the representative for all of mankind?

The covenant required that Adam obey and trust God entirely. In this, obedience would be rewarded with eternal life and blessing, but disobedience would be punished with curse and death. Adam disobeyed, bringing the consequences upon mankind.

Genesis 2:16-17 And the LORD God commanded the man, saying, "You may surely eat of every tree of the garden, but of the tree of the knowledge of good and evil you shall not eat, for in the day that you eat of it you shall surely die."

Ecclesiastes 7:29 ... God made man upright ...

Romans 6:23 For the wages of sin is death ...

Romans 5:12 (NASB) Therefore, just as through one man sin entered into the world, and death through sin, and so death spread to all men, because all sinned

Hosea 6:7 But like Adam they transgressed the covenant; there they dealt faithlessly with me.

This covenant is sometimes called the Covenant of Works, the Covenant of Obedience, the Covenant of Creation, the Adamic Covenant, or the Edenic Covenant.

Q58. What is the Old Covenant?

The Old Covenant was a temporary covenant made primarily with Israelites and was defined by the Abrahamic Covenant, conditioned by the Mosaic Covenant, and focused by the Davidic Covenant. This covenant offered temporary blessings but did not offer eternal life. Through promises, types, and shadows, it taught about the Messiah, who was to come to fulfill the law, establish the New Covenant, and redeem the elect.

Genesis 17:1-2 When Abram was ninety-nine years old the LORD appeared to Abram and said to him, "I am God Almighty; walk before me, and be blameless, that I may make my covenant between me and you, and may multiply you greatly."

Deuteronomy 11:26-28 "See, I am setting before you today a blessing and a curse: the blessing, if you obey the commandments of the LORD your God, which I command you today, and the curse, if you do not obey the commandments of the LORD your God, but turn aside from the way that I am commanding you today, to go after other gods that you have not known."

James 2:10 For whoever keeps the whole law but fails in one point has become accountable for all of it.

Hebrews 10:1 (NASB) For the Law, since it has only a shadow of the good things to come and not the very form of things, can never, by the same sacrifices which they offer continually year by year, make perfect those who draw near

(Further study: Hebrews 8:4-5; Romans 4:2-3, 13, 16; Acts 4:12; Genesis 12:1-3; 15:18–21; 17:1-14; 22:16-18; Exodus 19-24; 2 Samuel 7)

Q59. What is the New Covenant?

It is the covenant by which God saves the elect, by grace through faith in Jesus Christ. The New Covenant was planned before creation, promised in Genesis after the fall, and formally established by the blood of Christ when the work required of Him was complete.

Jeremiah 31:31 "Behold, the days are coming, declares the LORD, when I will make a new covenant with the house of Israel and the house of Judah"

Matthew 5:17 "Do not think that I have come to abolish the Law or the Prophets; I have not come to abolish them but to fulfill them."

Hebrews 8:6 But as it is, Christ has obtained a ministry that is as much more excellent than the old as the covenant he mediates is better, since it is enacted on better promises.

Luke 22:20 And likewise the cup after they had eaten, [Jesus said], "This cup that is poured out for you is the new covenant in my blood."

Hebrews 8:13 In speaking of a new covenant, he makes the first one obsolete. And what is becoming obsolete and growing old is ready to vanish away.

Hebrews 9:15 Therefore he is the mediator of a new covenant, so that those who are called may receive the promised eternal inheritance, since a death has occurred that redeems them from the transgressions committed under the first covenant.

Galatians 3:14 so that in Christ Jesus the blessing of Abraham might come to the Gentiles, so that we might receive the promised Spirit through faith.

(Further study: Genesis 3:15; Ezekiel 36:25-28; Jeremiah 31:31-34; Ephesians 2:11-22; Hebrews 8; John 10:27-30; Hebrews 9:28)

This covenant is sometimes called the Covenant of Grace.

Part 7:
Doctrine of Christ
(Christology)

Q60. Does Jesus now have a divine nature or a human nature?

At the incarnation, Jesus took on a human nature yet remained eternally, fully divine at the same time. Jesus Christ is one Person, fully God and fully man.

Hebrews 1:3 He is the radiance of the glory of God and the exact imprint of his nature, and he upholds the universe by the word of his power. After making purification for sins, he sat down at the right hand of the Majesty on high

Philippians 2:7-8 but made himself nothing, taking the form of a servant, being born in the likeness of men. And being found in human form, he humbled himself by becoming obedient to the point of death, even death on a cross.

Luke 1:35 And the angel answered her, "The Holy Spirit will come upon you, and the power of the Most High will overshadow you: therefore the child to be born will be called holy — the Son of God."

Matthew 1:23 "Behold, the virgin shall conceive and bear a son, and they shall call his name Immanuel" (which means, God with us).

Matthew 4:1 Then Jesus was led up by the Spirit into the wilderness to be tempted by the devil.

Humiliation of Christ: Jesus, in obedience to God the Father, took on human nature, came under the law, was tempted in this life, suffered the wrath of God by being cursed on the cross, and died a physical death.

Hypostatic Union: Jesus Christ's eternal, fully divine nature being united to His fully human nature at His incarnation. These two natures are not mixed, confused, or changed but are united without loss of separate identity, and they are inseparable.

Q61. What makes Christ's life different from every other person?

He was conceived in Mary by the Holy Spirit, and He obeyed God's law perfectly: He never sinned.

Matthew 1:20 ... "Joseph son of David, do not be afraid to take Mary home as your wife, because what is conceived in her is from the Holy Spirit."

1 Peter 2:22 [Jesus] committed no sin, neither was deceit found in his mouth.

Philippians 2:8 And being found in human form, he humbled himself by becoming obedient to the point of death, even death on a cross.

Hebrews 7:26 For it was indeed fitting that we should have such a high priest, holy, innocent, unstained, separated from sinners, and exalted above the heavens.

1 Peter 3:18 For Christ also suffered once for sins, the righteous for the unrighteous, that he might bring us to God, being put to death in the flesh but made alive in the spirit

Mark 10:45 "For even the Son of Man came not to be served but to serve, and to give his life as a ransom for many."

Q62. What did Christ accomplish by dying on the cross?

Substitutionary Atonement.
On the cross, Christ fully satisfied God's divine wrath as the perfect substitute in place of His elect.

2 Corinthians 5:21 (NASB) He made Him who knew no sin to be sin on our behalf, so that we might become the righteousness of God in Him.

Romans 3:25 ... God put forward [Jesus] as a propitiation by his blood, to be received by faith. This was to show God's righteousness ...

John 11:51-52 ... he prophesied that Jesus would die for the nation, and not for the nation only, but also to gather into one the children of God who are scattered abroad.

1 John 4:10 (NIV1984) This is love: not that we loved God, but that he loved us and sent his Son as an atoning sacrifice for our sins.

Romans 5:8 but God shows his love for us in that while we were still sinners, Christ died for us.

1 Peter 2:24 (NASB) and He Himself bore our sins in His body on the cross, so that we might die to sin and live to righteousness; for by His wounds you were healed.

Hebrews 9:22 Indeed, under the law almost everything is purified with blood, and without the shedding of blood there is no forgiveness of sins.

Q63. For whom did Christ die?
Christ died only for those people whom the Father had given Him: the elect.

Matthew 1:21 (NASB) "She will bear a Son; and you shall call His name Jesus, for He will save His people from their sins."

John 10:15, 25-30 (NASB) [Jesus said] "even as the Father knows Me and I know the Father; and I lay down My life for the sheep." ... "I told you, and you do not believe; the works that I do in My Father's name, these testify of Me. But you do not believe because you are not of My sheep. My sheep hear My voice, and I know them, and they follow Me; and I give eternal life to them, and they will never perish; and no one will snatch them out of My hand. My Father, who has given them to Me, is greater than all; and no one is able to snatch them out of the Father's hand. I and the Father are one."

John 6:37-40 (NASB) "All that the Father gives Me will come to Me, and the one who comes to Me I will certainly not cast out. For I have come down from heaven, not to do My own will, but the will of Him who sent Me. This is the will of Him who sent Me, that of all that He has given Me I lose nothing, but raise it up on the last day. For this is the will of My Father, that everyone who beholds the Son and believes in Him will have eternal life, and I Myself will raise him up on the last day."

John 17:9 "I am praying for them. I am not praying for the world but for those whom you have given me, for they are yours."

Ephesians 5:25 ... Christ loved the church and gave himself up for her

Limited Atonement (also known as Definite Atonement and Particular Atonement): Christ's work on the cross was not done for every human to ever live; rather, it was done exclusively for God's elect, who are chosen people from throughout all of human history and represent every tribe, tongue, and nation. In doing this, Christ accomplished substitutionary atonement for the chosen ones by cancelling the debt of all their sin, appeasing God's holy wrath, and earning all the benefits of their salvation.

Q64. Christ Jesus' body died on the cross, but did He remain dead?

No. On the third day, Christ rose physically from the grave!

Mark 8:31 And he began to teach them that the Son of Man must suffer many things ... and be killed, and after three days rise again.

Acts 2:24 God raised him up, loosing the pangs of death, because it was not possible for him to be held by it.

1 Corinthians 15:3-4 (NASB) For I delivered to you as of first importance what I also received, that Christ died for our sins according to the Scriptures, and that He was buried, and that He was raised on the third day according to the Scriptures

Matthew 28:6 "... he has risen, as he said ..."

John 20:27 Then [Jesus] said to Thomas, "Put your finger here, and see my hands; and put out your hand, and place it in my side. Do not disbelieve, but believe."

Q65. Why is it important that Jesus rose from the grave?

All authority for salvation is granted to Jesus in His resurrection. Without His resurrection, faith in Christ would be useless — no one would be redeemed from sin.

John 2:19 Jesus answered them, "Destroy this temple, and in three days I will raise it up."

Acts 2:24 God raised him up, loosing the pangs of death, because it was not possible for him to be held by it.

Acts 13:30, 38-39 "But God raised him from the dead," "Let it be known to you therefore, brothers, that through this man forgiveness of sins is proclaimed to you, and by him everyone who believes is freed from everything from which you could not be freed by the law of Moses."

1 Corinthians 15:14-20 (NASB) and if Christ has not been raised, then our preaching is vain, your faith also is vain. Moreover we are even found to be false witnesses of God, because we testified against God that He raised Christ, whom He did not raise, if in fact the dead are not raised. For if the dead are not raised, not even Christ has been raised; and if Christ has not been raised, your faith is worthless; you are still in your sins. Then those also who have fallen asleep in Christ have perished. If we have hoped in Christ in this life only, we are of all men most to be pitied. But now Christ has been raised from the dead, the first fruits of those who are asleep.

Romans 4:24-25 ... It will be counted to us who believe in him who raised from the dead Jesus our Lord, who was delivered up for our trespasses and raised for our justification.

Q66. Where is Jesus now?

Jesus is alive, and His body is exalted in heaven, where He is preparing a place for His redeemed people and interceding for them in the presence of God the Father.

Romans 8:34 Who is to condemn? Christ Jesus is the one who died — more than that, who was raised — who is at the right hand of God, who indeed is interceding for us.

Colossians 3:1 If then you have been raised with Christ, seek the things that are above, where Christ is, seated at the right hand of God.

1 John 2:1 My little children, I am writing these things to you so that you may not sin. But if anyone does sin, we have an advocate with the Father, Jesus Christ the righteous.

Hebrews 9:24 For Christ has entered, not into holy places made with hands, which are copies of the true things, but into heaven itself, now to appear in the presence of God on our behalf.

John 14:2-3 In my Father's house are many rooms. If it were not so, would I have told you that I go to prepare a place for you? And if I go and prepare a place for you, I will come again and will take you to myself, that where I am you may be also.

Romans 5:10 For if while we were enemies we were reconciled to God by the death of his Son, much more, now that we are reconciled, shall we be saved by his life.

Q67. When will Jesus return?

Jesus will physically return according to the will of God. Until then, we are commanded to be faithful servants and wise stewards. Come, Lord Jesus!

Matthew 24:36 "But concerning that day and hour no one knows, not even the angels of heaven, nor the Son, but the Father only."

Hebrews 9:28 so Christ, having been offered once to bear the sins of many, will appear a second time, not to deal with sin but to save those who are eagerly waiting for him.

1 Thessalonians 4:16 For the Lord himself will descend from heaven with a cry of command, with the voice of an archangel, and with the sound of the trumpet of God. And the dead in Christ will rise first.

Matthew 24:42, 44 "Therefore, stay awake, for you do not know on what day your Lord is coming. Therefore you also must be ready, for the Son of Man is coming at an hour you do not expect."

Revelation 22:20 He who testifies to these things says, "Surely I am coming soon." Amen. Come, Lord Jesus!

Q68. What is the gospel?

The gospel is the good news of the grace and power of God to redeem undeserving sinners to eternal life through Jesus' perfect, sinless life; substitutional, sacrificial death; and victorious resurrection from the grave. These sinners are saved by grace alone through faith alone in Jesus alone from the eternal wrath they deserved, and they are reconciled into an eternally secure relationship with God.

1 Corinthians 15:3-4 (NASB) For I delivered to you as of first importance what I also received, that Christ died for our sins according to the Scriptures, and that He was buried, and that He was raised on the third day according to the Scriptures

Romans 5:8 ... God shows his love for us in that while we were still sinners, Christ died for us.

John 3:16 (YLT) for God did so love the world, that His Son — the only begotten — He gave, that every one who is believing in him may not perish, but may have life [everlasting].

Ephesians 2:8-10 For by grace you have been saved through faith. And this is not your own doing; it is the gift of God, not a result of works, so that no one may boast. For we are his workmanship, created in Christ Jesus for good works, which God prepared beforehand, that we should walk in them.

Colossians 1:13-14 (NASB) For He rescued us from the domain of darkness, and transferred us to the kingdom of His beloved Son, in whom we have redemption, the forgiveness of sins.

1 Thessalonians 1:10 ... Jesus ... delivers us from the wrath to come.

Q69. How was Jesus our sacrifice?

Jesus is the spotless Lamb who took away our guilt from sin by having taken our place under the wrath of God.

Isaiah 53:5 But he was pierced for our transgressions; he was crushed for our iniquities; upon him was the chastisement that brought us peace, and with his wounds we are healed.

John 1:35-36 The next day again John was standing with two of his disciples, and he looked at Jesus as he walked by and said, "Behold, the Lamb of God!"

Romans 4:25 [Jesus] was delivered up for our trespasses and raised for our justification.

Hebrews 9:28 so Christ, having been offered once to bear the sins of many ...

1 Peter 2:24 (NASB) and He Himself bore our sins in His body on the cross, so that we might die to sin and live to righteousness; for by His wounds you were healed.

Hebrews 10:10 And by that will we have been sanctified through the offering of the body of Jesus Christ once for all.

Romans 8:3-4 (NASB) For what the Law could not do, weak as it was through the flesh, God did: sending His own Son in the likeness of sinful flesh and as an offering for sin, He condemned sin in the flesh, so that the requirement of the Law might be fulfilled in us, who do not walk according to the flesh but according to the Spirit.

Propitiation: Jesus satisfies God's wrath due the elect based on His substitutionary atonement.

Expiation: Jesus takes away the guilt of the elect based on His substitutionary atonement.

Q70. How is Jesus our righteousness?

His perfect life of obedience is credited to us. God sees Christ's righteousness when He looks on those who are saved.

Romans 1:16-17 For I am not ashamed of the gospel, for it is the power of God for salvation to everyone who believes, to the Jew first and also to the Greek. For in it the righteousness of God is revealed from faith for faith, as it is written, "The righteous shall live by faith."

1 Corinthians 1:30 And because of him you are in Christ Jesus, who became to us wisdom from God, righteousness and sanctification and redemption

Philippians 3:9 and be found in [Jesus], not having a righteousness of my own that comes from the law, but that which comes through faith in Christ, the righteousness from God that depends on faith

Romans 4:25 [Jesus] was delivered up for our trespasses and raised for our justification.

Romans 4:3-6 (NASB) For what does the Scripture say? "ABRAHAM BELIEVED GOD, AND IT WAS CREDITED TO HIM AS RIGHTEOUSNESS." Now to the one who works, his wage is not credited as a favor, but as what is due. But to the one who does not work, but believes in Him who justifies the ungodly, his faith is credited as righteousness, just as David also speaks of the blessing on the man to whom God credits righteousness apart from works

Imputation: When something not of your own is credited (accounted) to you. Adam's guilt was imputed to all persons. The sin of the elect was imputed to Jesus at the cross, and Jesus' perfect righteousness is imputed to the elect at conversion.

Justification: God declares a believer *not guilty* based on the believer being credited Jesus Christ's perfect righteousness.

Q71. How is Jesus our reconciliation?

By satisfying God's wrath due our sin, He restores our relationship with God.

Romans 5:1 Therefore, since we have been justified by faith, we have peace with God through our Lord Jesus Christ.

1 Timothy 2:5 For there is one God and one mediator between God and men, the man Christ Jesus

Romans 5:11 ... we also rejoice in God through our Lord Jesus Christ, through whom we have now received reconciliation.

2 Corinthians 5:18 All this is from God, who through Christ reconciled us to himself and gave us the ministry of reconciliation

Q72. How is Jesus our victory?

He has defeated Satan, sin, and death for us;
therefore, we are no longer enslaved to these.

Colossians 2:15 He [God] disarmed the rulers and authorities and put them to open shame, by triumphing over them in him [Jesus].

Hebrews 2:14-15 (NASB) Therefore, since the children share in flesh and blood, He Himself [Jesus] likewise also partook of the same, that through death He might render powerless him who had the power of death, that is, the devil, and might free those who through fear of death were subject to slavery all their lives.

2 Timothy 1:10 (NASB) ... [Christ Jesus] abolished death and brought life and immortality to light through the gospel

1 Corinthians 15:56-57 The sting of death is sin, and the power of sin is the law. But thanks be to God, who gives us the victory through our Lord Jesus Christ.

Romans 6:6 We know that our old self was crucified with him in order that the body of sin might be brought to nothing, so that we would no longer be enslaved to sin.

Romans 6:17-18 But thanks be to God, that you who were once slaves of sin have become obedient from the heart to the standard of teaching to which you were committed, and, having been set free from sin, have become slaves of righteousness.

Romans 16:20 The God of peace will soon crush Satan under your feet. The grace of our Lord Jesus Christ be with you.

1 Corinthians 15:26 The last enemy to be destroyed is death.

Q73. What three offices does Christ fulfill as our promised redeemer?

Christ fulfills the offices of Prophet, Priest, and King.

Deuteronomy 18:15 "The LORD your God will raise up for you a prophet like me from among you from you brothers — it is to him you shall listen"

Hebrews 6:20 where Jesus has gone as a forerunner on our behalf, having become a high priest forever after the order of Melchizedek.

Matthew 21:5 "Say to the daughter of Zion, 'Behold, your king is coming to you, humble, and mounted on a donkey, on a colt, the foal of a beast of burden.'"

Q74. How is Christ our Prophet?

Christ is our Prophet by revealing God's will to us through His word, affirmed by the Holy Spirit.

John 6:63 "... The words that I have spoken to you are spirit and life."

1 Peter 2:22 [Jesus] committed no sin, neither was deceit found in his mouth.

John 8:28 (NASB) So Jesus said, "When you lift up the Son of Man, then you will know that I am He, and I do nothing on My own initiative, but I speak these things as the Father taught Me."

John 7:16 (NASB) So Jesus answered them and said, "My teaching is not Mine, but His who sent Me."

John 17:8 (NASB) "for the words which You gave Me I have given to them; and they received them and truly understood that I came forth from You, and they believed that You sent Me."

Acts 2:22 (NASB) "Men of Israel, listen to these words: Jesus the Nazarene, a man attested to you by God with miracles and wonders and signs which God performed through Him in your midst, just as you yourselves know"

Deuteronomy 18:18 (NASB) "I will raise up a prophet from among their countrymen like you, and I will put My words in his mouth, and he shall speak to them all that I command him."

Acts 3:22-23 (NASB) "Moses said, 'THE LORD GOD WILL RAISE UP FOR YOU A PROPHET LIKE ME FROM YOUR BRETHREN; TO HIM YOU SHALL GIVE HEED to everything He says to you. And it will be that every soul that does not heed that prophet shall be utterly destroyed from among the people.'"

John 14:26 (NASB) "But the Helper, the Holy Spirit, whom the Father will send in My name, He will teach you all things, and bring to your remembrance all that I said to you."

Q75. How is Christ our Priest?

Christ is our Priest because He gave Himself as a sacrifice in our place to satisfy the wrath of God, and He is in continual intercession to God the Father on our behalf.

Romans 8:34 Who is to condemn? Christ Jesus is the one who died—more than that, who was raised—who is at the right hand of God, who indeed is interceding for us.

Hebrews 7:23-28 (NASB) The former priests, on the one hand, existed in greater numbers because they were prevented by death from continuing, but Jesus, on the other hand, because He continues forever, holds His priesthood permanently. Therefore He is able also to save forever those who draw near to God through Him, since He always lives to make intercession for them. For it was fitting for us to have such a high priest, holy, innocent, undefiled, separated from sinners and exalted above the heavens; who does not need daily, like those high priests, to offer up sacrifices, first for His own sins and then for the sins of the people, because this He did once for all when He offered up Himself. For the Law appoints men as high priests who are weak, but the word of the oath, which came after the Law, appoints a Son, made perfect forever.

1 Timothy 2:5-6 For there is one God, and there is one mediator between God and men, the man Christ Jesus who gave himself as a ransom for all, which is the testimony given at the proper time.

Hebrews 4:14-16 (NASB) Therefore, since we have a great high priest who has passed through the heavens, Jesus the Son of God, let us hold fast our confession. For we do not have a high priest who cannot sympathize with our weaknesses, but One who has been tempted in all things as we are, yet without sin. Therefore let us draw near with confidence to the throne of grace, so that we may receive mercy and find grace to help in time of need.

Hebrews 9:28 so Christ, having been offered once to bear the sins of many, will appear a second time, not to deal with sin but to save those who are eagerly waiting for him.

Q76. How is Christ our King?

Christ is our King by subduing and ruling over all the Father has given Him.

John 18:37 (NASB) Therefore Pilate said to Him, "So You are a king?" Jesus answered, "You say correctly that I am a king. For this I have been born, and for this I have come into the world, to testify to the truth. Everyone who is of the truth hears My voice."

Ephesians 1:20-23 that [God the Father] worked in Christ when he raised him from the dead and seated him at his right hand in the heavenly places, far above all rule and authority and power and dominion, and above every name that is named, not only in this age but also in the one to come. And he put all things under his feet and gave him as head over all things to the church, which is his body, the fullness of him who fills all in all.

Revelation 17:14 (NASB) "These will wage war against the Lamb, and the Lamb will overcome them, because He is Lord of lords and King of kings, and those who are with Him are the called and chosen and faithful."

Revelation 19:16 (NASB) And on His robe and on His thigh He has a name written, "KING OF KINGS, AND LORD OF LORDS."

Isaiah 33:22 For the LORD is our judge; the LORD is our lawgiver; the LORD is our king; he will save us.

2 Samuel 7:12-13 (NASB) "When your days are complete and you lie down with your fathers, I will raise up your descendant after you, who will come forth from you, and I will establish his kingdom. He shall build a house for My name, and I will establish the throne of his kingdom forever."

Acts 2:30 "Being therefore a prophet, and knowing that God had sworn with an oath to him that he would set one of his descendants on his throne"

1 Timothy 6:15 which he will display at the proper time—he who is the blessed and only Sovereign, the King of kings and Lord of lords

Part 8:
Doctrine of Salvation
(Soteriology)

Q77. Why did God ordain creation and the plan of salvation?

God ordained creation and the plan of salvation for the display of His glory, highlighting especially His grace and power.

Romans 11:36 (NASB) For from Him and through Him and to Him are all things. To Him be the glory forever. Amen.

Romans 9:22-23 What if God, desiring to show his wrath and to make known his power, has endured with much patience vessels of wrath prepared for destruction, in order to make known the riches of his glory for vessels of mercy, which he has prepared beforehand for glory

Psalm 76:10 Surely the wrath of man shall praise you; the remnant of wrath you will put on like a belt.

Ephesians 1:5-6 he predestined us for adoption as sons through Jesus Christ, according to the purpose of his will, to the praise of his glorious grace, with which he has blessed us in the Beloved.

Ephesians 2:7 so that in the coming ages he might show the immeasurable riches of his grace in kindness toward us in Christ Jesus.

Philippians 1:9-11 (NASB) And this I pray, that your love may abound still more and more in real knowledge and all discernment, so that you may approve the things that are excellent, in order to be sincere and blameless until the day of Christ; having been filled with the fruit of righteousness which comes through Jesus Christ, to the glory and praise of God.

2 Corinthians 12:9 (NASB) And He has said to me, "My grace is sufficient for you, for power is perfected in weakness." Most gladly, therefore, I will rather boast about my weaknesses, so that the power of Christ may dwell in me.

(Further study: Ephesians 1:11-14; 2 Corinthians 4:15; 1 Peter 2:9; 1 Corinthians 2:1-5; Colossians 1:16)

Q78. Who will be saved?

Only those whom God has chosen for salvation — the elect — will be saved.

Ephesians 1:4-5 even as he chose us in him before the foundation of the world, that we should be holy and blameless before him. In love he predestined us for adoption as sons through Jesus Christ, according to the purpose of his will

Romans 11:5-7 So too, at the present time there is a remnant chosen by grace. And if by grace, then it cannot be based on works; if it were, grace would no longer be grace. What then? What the people of Israel sought so earnestly they did not obtain. The elect among them did, but the others were hardened

Romans 9:11 though they were not yet born and had done nothing either good or bad — in order that God's purpose of election might continue, not because of works but because of him who calls

Romans 9:16 So then it depends not on human will or exertion, but on God, who has mercy.

2 Timothy 1:8-10 (NASB) Therefore do not be ashamed of the testimony of our Lord or of me His prisoner, but join with me in suffering for the gospel according to the power of God, who has saved us and called us with a holy calling, not according to our works, but according to His own purpose and grace which was granted us in Christ Jesus from all eternity, but now has been revealed by the appearing of our Savior Christ Jesus, who abolished death and brought life and immortality to light through the gospel

(Further study: Romans 9; 1 Corinthians 1:27-29; Ephesians 1; John 17:1-5; 1 Peter 2:9; 1 Peter 1:1-2; 2 Peter 1:10; Proverbs 16:4; 1 Peter 2:8; Jude 1:4; Colossians 3:12-13)

Unconditional Individual Election: Before creation existed, God chose which individual human beings would receive salvation from sin, death, and God's eternal wrath. This choice to redeem certain ones is not based on any so-called goodness, will, or work in them; rather, it is based on the freedom and grace of God in Christ Jesus alone.

Q79. When did God choose individuals for salvation?

Based on His will alone, in love, God chose and predestined each of the elect before creation.

Romans 8:29-30 (NASB) For those whom He foreknew, He also predestined to become conformed to the image of His Son, so that He would be the firstborn among many brethren; and these whom He predestined, He also called; and these whom He called, He also justified; and these whom He justified, He also glorified.

Revelation 13:8 and all who dwell on earth will worship it [satanic beast], everyone whose name has not been written before the foundation of the world in the book of life of the Lamb who was slain.

Ephesians 1:4-5 even as he chose us in him before the foundation of the world, that we should be holy and blameless before him. In love he predestined us for adoption as sons through Jesus Christ, according to the purpose of his will

Ephesians 1:11 In him we have obtained an inheritance, having been predestined according to the purpose of him who works all things according to the counsel of his will

2 Timothy 1:9 who saved us and called us to a holy calling, not because of our works but because of his own purpose and grace, which he gave us in Christ Jesus before the ages began

Predestination: In love, based on the perfect will of the Triune God, the destiny of salvation unto eternal life for God's chosen people was planned and ordained from start to end before creation began. Predestination is not based on foreseen deeds or faith in anyone; it is based on God's will alone.

Q80. What is saving grace?

Saving grace is God's love, forgiveness, and redemption freely and effectively given in Jesus to the elect, who are undeserving of this.

Ephesians 2:8-9 For by grace you have been saved through faith. And this is not your own doing; it is the gift of God, not a result of works, so that no one may boast.

Ephesians 1:6 to the praise of his glorious grace, with which he has blessed us in the Beloved.

John 1:17 For the law was given through Moses; grace and truth came through Jesus Christ.

Romans 11:6 But if it is by grace, it is no longer on the basis of works; otherwise grace would no longer be grace.

Grace: Unmerited favor (or an undeserved gift) given by an unobligated giver.

Q81. What is opposed to God's grace?

Opposed to God's grace are the lies that we are worthy or that we can work hard enough to earn God's love and forgiveness or that we can seek, will, or choose Jesus without the Holy Spirit giving us new life and saving faith.

Romans 3:10-12 as it is written: "None is righteous, no, not one; no one understands; no one seeks for God. All have turned aside; together they have become worthless; no one does good, not even one."

Romans 3:20 For by works of the law no human being will be justified in his sight, since through the law comes knowledge of sin.

Romans 8:7-8 For the mind that is set on the flesh is hostile to God, for it does not submit to God's law; indeed, it cannot. Those who are in the flesh cannot please God.

Ephesians 2:8-9 For by grace you have been saved through faith. And this is not your own doing; it is the gift of God, not a result of works, so that no one may boast.

Romans 11:6 But if it is by grace, it is no longer on the basis of works; otherwise grace would no longer be grace.

Galatians 2:21 I do not nullify the grace of God, for if righteousness were through the law, then Christ died for no purpose.

John 6:63 "It is the Spirit who gives life; the flesh is no help at all. The words that I have spoken to you are spirit and life."

Romans 9:16 So then it depends not on human will or exertion, but on God, who has mercy.

(Further study: Luke 18:9-14)

Q82. How does God ordain His good news of salvation to be spread?

God commands His saved saints to faithfully proclaim the gospel of Jesus Christ to all people everywhere, unto the ends of the earth.

Matthew 4:17 From that time Jesus began to preach, saying, "Repent, for the kingdom of heaven is at hand."

Acts 16:30-31 (NASB) and after he brought them out, he said, "Sirs, what must I do to be saved?" They said, "Believe in the Lord Jesus, and you will be saved ..."

John 10:24-26 (NASB) The Jews then gathered around Him, and were saying to Him, "How long will You keep us in suspense? If You are the Christ, tell us plainly." Jesus answered them, "I told you, and you do not believe; the works that I do in My Father's name, these testify of Me. But you do not believe because you are not of My sheep."

Romans 10:14-17 (NASB) How then will they call on Him in whom they have not believed? How will they believe in Him whom they have not heard? And how will they hear without a preacher? How will they preach unless they are sent? Just as it is written, "HOW BEAUTIFUL ARE THE FEET OF THOSE WHO BRING GOOD NEWS OF GOOD THINGS!" However, they did not all heed the good news; for Isaiah says, "LORD, WHO HAS BELIEVED OUR REPORT?" So faith comes from hearing, and hearing by the word of Christ.

Acts 17:30 "... [God] commands all people everywhere to repent"

Matthew 22:14 "For many are called, but few are chosen."

General Gospel Call: The gospel of Jesus Christ being proclaimed to all tribes, tongues, and nations. God has ordained that gospel proclamation is the vehicle by which He sets the table for salvation.

Q83. Can people respond to the gospel by their own power, will, or choice?

No. Since the fall, we are all born spiritually dead in sin and unable to truly will or choose to have saving faith in Jesus. We need the Holy Spirit to first give us new life and the gift of saving faith.

1 Corinthians 15:22 (NASB) For as in Adam all die ...

Psalm 51:5 Behold, I was brought forth in iniquity, and in sin did my mother conceive me.

Genesis 6:5 The LORD saw that the wickedness of man was great in the earth, and that every intention of the thoughts of his heart was only evil continually.

John 8:34 (NASB) Jesus answered them, "Truly, truly, I say to you, everyone who commits sin is the slave of sin."

Romans 3:10-12 ... "None is righteous, no, not one; no one understands; no one seeks for God. All have turned aside; together they have become worthless; no one does good, not even one."

Romans 8:7-8 For the mind that is set on the flesh is hostile to God, for it does not submit to God's law; indeed, it cannot. Those who are in the flesh cannot please God.

1 Corinthians 2:14 The natural person does not accept the things of the Spirit of God, for they are folly to him, and he is not able to understand them because they are spiritually discerned.

John 6:44, 63, 65 "No one can come to me unless the Father who sent me draws him. And I will raise him up on the last day." "It is the Spirit who gives life; the flesh is no help at all. The words that I have spoken to you are spirit and life." ... "This is why I told you that no one can come to me unless it is granted him by the Father."

Ephesians 2:5 even when we were dead in our trespasses, [God] made us alive together with Christ—by grace you have been saved

Romans 9:16 So then it depends not on human will or exertion, but on God, who has mercy.

(See Glossary terms *Total Depravity, Human Inability,* and *Effective Call*)

Q84. How does a person change from spiritually dead to spiritually alive?

By God's will alone and according to His sovereign timing, the Holy Spirit causes each elect person to be born again, giving new life and saving faith in Jesus.

John 3:3, 7-8 (NASB) Jesus answered and said to him, "Truly, truly, I say to you, unless one is born again he cannot see the kingdom of God." "Do not be amazed that I said to you, 'You must be born again.' The wind blows where it wishes and you hear the sound of it, but do not know where it comes from and where it is going; so is everyone who is born of the Spirit."

John 6:63 "It is the Spirit who gives life; the flesh is no help at all."

Ezekiel 36:25-27 (NASB) "Then I will sprinkle clean water on you, and you will be clean; I will cleanse you from all your filthiness and from all your idols. Moreover, I will give you a new heart and put a new spirit within you; and I will remove the heart of stone from your flesh and give you a heart of flesh. I will put My Spirit within you and cause you to walk in My statutes, and you will be careful to observe My ordinances."

Ephesians 2:8-9 For by grace you have been saved through faith. And this is not your own doing; it is the gift of God, not a result of works, so that no one may boast.

Titus 3:5 he saved us, not because of works done by us in righteousness, but according to his own mercy, by the washing of regeneration and renewal of the Holy Spirit

1 Peter 1:3 (NASB) Blessed be the God and Father of our Lord Jesus Christ, who according to His great mercy has caused us to be born again to a living hope through the resurrection of Jesus Christ from the dead

(Further study: 2 Cor 5:17; John 1:12-13; James 1:18; Acts 16:14)

Regeneration (New Birth, Becoming Born Again): The act by which God, by His power and will, gives new life to the spiritually dead. Regeneration immediately precedes the gift of saving faith.

Q85. Who will respond to the gospel?
Those for whom Christ died — the elect — are each regenerated in God's sovereign timing and caused to respond.

John 6:44, 63, 65 "No one can come to me unless the Father who sent me draws him. And I will raise him up on the last day." "It is the Spirit who gives life; the flesh is no help at all. The words that I have spoken to you are spirit and life." And he said, "This is why I told you that no one can come to me unless it is granted him by the Father."

John 10:27 (NASB) "My sheep hear My voice, and I know them, and they follow Me."

John 10:3 "... The sheep hear his voice, and he calls his own sheep by name and leads them out."

Romans 8:30 (NASB) and these whom He predestined, He also called; and these whom He called, He also justified; and these whom He justified, He also glorified.

John 3:5-8 (NASB) Jesus answered, "Truly, truly, I say to you, unless one is born of water and the Spirit he cannot enter into the kingdom of God. That which is born of the flesh is flesh, and that which is born of the Spirit is spirit. Do not be amazed that I said to you, 'You must be born again.' The wind blows where it wishes and you hear the sound of it, but do not know where it comes from and where it is going; so is everyone who is born of the Spirit."

2 Thessalonians 2:14 To this he called you through our gospel, so that you may obtain the glory of our Lord Jesus Christ.

Effective Call (Irresistible Grace): The act of God in which He graciously summons each of the elect to Himself, regenerates them, and gives saving faith, so they willingly respond with genuine repentance and trust in Jesus Christ. God's effective call — saving grace — always brings about the response it demands in people's hearts.

Q86. What must we do to be saved?

When we are enabled by the power and will of God, we joyfully and willingly turn from sin and trust in Christ Jesus alone. This is saving faith.

John 3:16 (YLT) for God did so love the world, that His Son — the only begotten — He gave, that every one who is believing in him may not perish, but may have life [everlasting].

Matthew 4:17 From that time Jesus began to preach, saying, "Repent, for the kingdom of heaven is at hand."

Acts 16:30-31 (NASB) and after he brought them out, he said, "Sirs, what must I do to be saved?" They said, "Believe in the Lord Jesus, and you will be saved ..."

Mark 1:15 ... "The time is fulfilled, and the kingdom of God is at hand; repent and believe in the gospel."

Acts 17:30 "... [God] commands all people everywhere to repent"

John 10:27-28 (NASB) "My sheep hear My voice, and I know them, and they follow Me; and I give eternal life to them, and they will never perish; and no one will snatch them out of My hand."

Ephesians 2:8-9 For by grace you have been saved through faith. And this is not your own doing; it is the gift of God, not a result of works, so that no one may boast.

Romans 9:16 So then it depends not on human will or exertion, but on God, who has mercy.

Conversion: As a result of regeneration, God immediately gives the gift of saving faith by which a person willingly repents of sin and trusts his/her life and salvation to Jesus Christ alone.

Saving Faith: Rather than trusting one's own assumed worth, works, or ability, a person repents and believes that Jesus is God, trusts in Jesus' sinless life of perfect obedience, Jesus' sacrificial death on the cross in his/her place, and Jesus' rising from the dead to claim salvation and victory for him/her. Saving faith is produced in the elect by God and is always accompanied by progressive sanctification and ongoing repentance from sin.

Q87. What is turning from sin called?

Turning from sin is called repentance.
In light of the gospel, repentance is to turn
away from sin, including self-reign, and we
turn instead to Jesus Christ as our Savior and
the Lord of our lives.

Luke 24:46-47 (NASB) [Jesus] said to them, "Thus it is written, that the Christ would suffer and rise again from the dead the third day, and that repentance for forgiveness of sins would be proclaimed in His name to all the nations, beginning from Jerusalem."

Acts 11:18 When they heard these things they fell silent. And they glorified God, saying, "Then to the Gentiles also God has granted repentance that leads to life."

Acts 2:38 And Peter said to them, "Repent and be baptized every one of you in the name of Jesus Christ for the forgiveness of your sins ..."

Luke 13:5 "... unless you repent, you will all likewise perish."

Acts 17:30-31 "... [God] commands all people everywhere to repent, because he has fixed a day on which he will judge the world in righteousness by a man whom he has appointed; and of this he has given assurance to all by raising him from the dead."

2 Timothy 2:24-26 And the Lord's servant must not be quarrelsome but kind to everyone, able to teach, patiently enduring evil, correcting his opponents with gentleness. God may perhaps grant them repentance leading to a knowledge of the truth, and they may come to their senses and escape from the snare of the devil, after being captured by him to do his will.

Isaiah 6:5, 8 And I said: "Woe is me! For I am lost; for I am a man of unclean lips, and I dwell in the midst of a people of unclean lips; for my eyes have seen the King, the Lord of hosts!" And I heard the voice of the Lord saying, "Whom shall I send, and who will go for us?" Then I said, "Here I am! Send me."

Romans 6:22 ... now that you have been set free from sin and have become slaves of God ...

Q88. What does it mean to trust only in Jesus Christ?

It is to believe (trust) in the deity and work of Jesus Christ, rather than trusting one's own assumed worth, works, will, or ability.

John 14:6 Jesus said to him, "I am the way, and the truth, and the life. No one comes to the Father except through me."

Acts 16:31 ... "Believe in the Lord Jesus, and you will be saved ..."

Romans 10:9-10 ... if you confess with your mouth that Jesus is Lord and believe in your heart that God raised him from the dead, you will be saved. For with the heart one believes and is justified, and with the mouth one confesses and is saved.

Romans 3:20 For by works of the law no human being will be justified in his sight, since through the law comes knowledge of sin.

Ephesians 2:8-9 For by grace you have been saved through faith. And this is not your own doing; it is the gift of God, not a result of works, so that no one may boast.

Galatians 2:21 I do not nullify the grace of God, for if righteousness were through the law, then Christ died for no purpose.

Romans 11:6 But if it is by grace, it is no longer on the basis of works; otherwise grace would no longer be grace.

Q89. What do we receive when we are saved?

Among other blessings, we receive the forgiveness of all our sins, justification, reconciliation, adoption, and eternal life with Jesus, having now been sealed by the Holy Spirit.

Colossians 1:13-14 (NASB) For He rescued us from the domain of darkness, and transferred us to the kingdom of His beloved Son, in whom we have redemption, the forgiveness of sins.

Romans 5:1 Therefore, since we have been justified by faith, we have peace with God through our Lord Jesus Christ.

1 John 5:11 And this is the testimony, that God gave us eternal life, and this life is in his Son.

Romans 6:23 For the wages of sin is death, but the free gift of God is eternal life in Christ Jesus our Lord.

Ephesians 1:13-14 In him you also, when you heard the word of truth, the gospel of your salvation, and believed in him, were sealed with the promised Holy Spirit, who is the guarantee of our inheritance until we acquire possession of it, to the praise of his glory.

2 Corinthians 1:22 and [God] has also put his seal on us and given us his Spirit in our hearts as a guarantee.

Q90. What is justification?

Justification is the legal declaration in which God declares a believer not guilty based on the believer being credited Jesus Christ's perfect righteousness.

Ephesians 2:8-9 For by grace you have been saved through faith. And this is not your own doing; it is the gift of God, not a result of works, so that no one may boast.

Philippians 3:9 (NASB) and may be found in Him, not having a righteousness of my own derived from the Law, but that which is through faith in Christ, the righteousness which comes from God on the basis of faith

Romans 5:1 Therefore, since we have been justified by faith, we have peace with God through our Lord Jesus Christ.

2 Corinthians 5:21 (NASB) He made Him who knew no sin to be sin on our behalf, so that we might become the righteousness of God in Him.

Romans 4:3-6 (NASB) For what does the Scripture say? "ABRAHAM BELIEVED GOD, AND IT WAS CREDITED TO HIM AS RIGHTEOUSNESS." Now to the one who works, his wage is not credited as a favor, but as what is due. But to the one who does not work, but believes in Him who justifies the ungodly, his faith is credited as righteousness, just as David also speaks of the blessing on the man to whom God credits righteousness apart from works

Q91. What is adoption?

Adoption is the gracious act of God in which He makes a believer one of His children, giving the privileges of sonship.

Galatians 3:26 for in Christ Jesus you are all sons of God, through faith.

Galatians 4:4-5 But when the fullness of time had come, God sent forth his Son, born of woman, born under the law, to redeem those who were under the law, so that we might receive adoption as sons.

Romans 8:14-17 For all who are led by the Spirit of God are sons of God. For you did not receive the spirit of slavery to fall back into fear, but you have received the Spirit of adoption as sons, by whom we cry, "Abba! Father!" The Spirit himself bears witness with our spirit that we are children of God, and if children, then heirs — heirs of God and fellow heirs with Christ, provided we suffer with him in order that we may also be glorified with him.

John 1:12-13 But to all who did receive him, who believed in his name, he gave the right to become children of God, who were born, not of blood nor of the will of the flesh nor of the will of man, but of God.

1 John 3:1-2 (NASB) See how great a love the Father has bestowed on us, that we would be called children of God; and such we are. For this reason the world does not know us, because it did not know Him. Beloved, now we are children of God, and it has not appeared as yet what we will be. We know that when He appears, we will be like Him, because we will see Him just as He is.

Ephesians 1:4-5 even as he chose us in him before the foundation of the world, that we should be holy and blameless before him. In love he predestined us for adoption as sons through Jesus Christ, according to the purpose of his will

Q92. Is the Triune God united in providing salvation for the elect?

Yes. Based on God having one eternal will, each of the three Persons carries out the same plan of salvation and judgment. God the Father chose the elect before the foundation of the world, Jesus died exclusively for those elect people, and the Holy Spirit only regenerates those same elect people.

Luke 10:21 In that same hour he rejoiced in the Holy Spirit and said, "I thank you, Father, Lord of heaven and earth, that you have hidden these things from the wise and understanding and revealed them to little children; yes, Father, for such was your gracious will."

Ephesians 1:4-5 ... [God] chose us in him before the foundation of the world, that we should be holy and blameless before him. In love he predestined us ...

John 10:15, 25-30 (NASB) [Jesus said] "... I lay down My life for the sheep" ... "I told you, and you do not believe; the works that I do in My Father's name, these testify of Me. But you do not believe because you are not of My sheep. My sheep hear My voice, and I know them, and they follow Me; and I give eternal life to them, and they will never perish; and no one will snatch them out of My hand. My Father, who has given them to Me, is greater than all; and no one is able to snatch them out of the Father's hand. I and the Father are one."

Ephesians 5:25 ... Christ loved the church and gave himself up for her

Titus 3:5 he saved us, not because of works done by us in righteousness, but according to his own mercy, by the washing of regeneration and renewal of the Holy Spirit

Part 9:
Doctrine of the Holy Spirit (Pneumatology)

Q93. What is the indwelling of the Holy Spirit, and when does it happen?

The indwelling of the Holy Spirit is the action by which God takes up permanent residence in the body of an elect person at regeneration.

John 3:5 (NASB) Jesus answered, "Truly, truly, I say to you, unless one is born of water and the Spirit he cannot enter into the kingdom of God."

Ezekiel 36:25-27 (NASB) "Then I will sprinkle clean water on you, and you will be clean; I will cleanse you from all your filthiness and from all your idols. Moreover, I will give you a new heart and put a new spirit within you; and I will remove the heart of stone from your flesh and give you a heart of flesh. I will put My Spirit within you and cause you to walk in My statutes, and you will be careful to observe My ordinances."

1 Corinthians 6:19 Or do you not know that your body is a temple of the Holy Spirit within you, whom you have from God? ...

John 14:17 "even the Spirit of truth, whom the world cannot receive, because it neither sees him nor knows him. You know him, for he dwells with you and will be in you."

Galatians 4:6 And because you are sons, God has sent the Spirit of his son into our hearts, crying, "Abba! Father!"

Romans 8:11 If the Spirit of him who raised Jesus from the dead dwells in you, he who raised Christ Jesus from the dead will also give life to your mortal bodies through his Spirit who dwells in you.

Q94. Can a true Christian abandon or lose his/her salvation?

No. Everyone who has been truly born again will persevere in saving faith forever by the power and work of the Holy Spirit. God will lose none of those He saves.

Philippians 1:6 And I am sure of this, that he who began a good work in you will bring it to completion at the day of Jesus Christ.

1 Peter 1:3-5 (NASB) Blessed be the God and Father of our Lord Jesus Christ, who according to His great mercy has caused us to be born again to a living hope through the resurrection of Jesus Christ from the dead, to obtain an inheritance which is imperishable and undefiled and will not fade away, reserved in heaven for you, who are protected by the power of God through faith for a salvation ready to be revealed in the last time.

Jeremiah 32:40 "'I will make with them an everlasting covenant, that I will not turn away from doing good to them. And I will put the fear of me in their hearts, that they may not turn from me.'"

2 Corinthians 1:21-22 And it is God who establishes us with you in Christ, and has anointed us, and who has also put his seal on us and given us his Spirit in our hearts as a guarantee.

Romans 8:38-39 (NASB) For I am convinced that neither death, nor life, nor angels, nor principalities, nor things present, nor things to come, nor powers, nor height, nor depth, nor any other created thing, will be able to separate us from the love of God, which is in Christ Jesus our Lord

(Further study: John 10:27-30; John 6:37-40; Ephesians 1:13-14)

Perseverance of the Saints: God keeps His saved people forever. The elect are saved and eternally secure by God's power and promise. Because of grace, God works so those whom He has chosen and given eternal salvation, by the power and work of the Holy Spirit, are enabled to persevere in faith forever. A person shows that he/she was truly saved by God by persevering in faith in Christ until the end.

Q95. In addition to being the seal of our salvation, what is the Holy Spirit's ongoing ministry to the saved?

The Holy Spirit enables us to understand God's word, convicts us of sin, comforts us, prays for us, leads us, gives us spiritual gifts, and causes in us increasing desire and ability to obey God.

John 14:26 (NASB) "But the Helper, the Holy Spirit, whom the Father will send in My name, He will teach you all things, and bring to your remembrance all that I said to you."

Romans 8:26 Likewise the Spirit helps us in our weakness. For we do not know what to pray for as we ought, but the Spirit himself intercedes for us with groanings too deep for words.

Romans 8:14 For all who are led by the Spirit of God are sons of God.

1 Corinthians 12:4-7, 11 Now there are varieties of gifts, but the same Spirit; and there are varieties of service, but the same Lord; and there are varieties of activities, but it is the same God who empowers them all in everyone. To each is given the manifestation of the Spirit for the common good. All these are empowered by one and the same Spirit, who apportions to each one individually as he wills

Q96. By what evidence does one show true saving faith?

By the work of God's power and grace, the saved imperfectly but increasingly show the fruit of the Spirit, repent from sin, affirm biblical truth, grow in holiness by obeying God's word, love others, live within Christian community, and abide in Christ by persevering in saving faith.

Philippians 1:6 And I am sure of this, that he who began a good work in you will bring it to completion at the day of Jesus Christ.

Galatians 5:22-23 But the fruit of the Spirit is love, joy, peace, patience, kindness, goodness, faithfulness, gentleness, self-control; against such things there is no law.

Matthew 3:8 "Bear fruit in keeping with repentance."

2 Timothy 2:15 Do your best to present yourself to God as one approved, a worker who has no need to be ashamed, rightly handling the word of truth.

John 14:15 "If you love me, you will keep my commandments."

James 2:17-18 So also faith by itself, if it does not have works, is dead ... I will show you my faith by my works.

Matthew 22:39 "... You shall love your neighbor as yourself."

Hebrews 3:13 But exhort one another every day, as long as it is called "today," that none of you may be hardened by the deceitfulness of sin.

Colossians 1:23 if indeed you continue in the faith, stable and steadfast, not shifting from the hope of the gospel that you heard ...

John 3:16 (YLT) for God did so love the world, that His Son—the only begotten—He gave, that every one who is believing in him may not perish, but may have life [everlasting].

Q97. What is progressive sanctification?

Progressive sanctification is growing in holiness through obedience to the Lordship of Jesus and His word from a right heart. By grace, it is a lifelong process powered by the Holy Spirit to change us to become more like Christ.

Colossians 1:28 Him we proclaim, warning everyone and teaching everyone with all wisdom, that we may present everyone mature in Christ.

Philippians 2:12-13 Therefore, my beloved, as you have always obeyed, so now, not only as in my presence but much more in my absence, work out your own salvation with fear and trembling, for it is God who works in you, both to will and to work for his good pleasure.

1 Corinthians 15:10 But by the grace of God I am what I am, and his grace toward me was not in vain. On the contrary, I worked harder than any of them, though it was not I, but the grace of God that is with me.

Romans 12:2 Do not be conformed to this world, but be transformed by the renewal of your mind, that by testing you may discern what is the will of God, what is good and acceptable and perfect.

1 Peter 1:13-16 Therefore, preparing your minds for action, and being sober-minded, set your hope fully on the grace that will be brought to you at the revelation of Jesus Christ. As obedient children, do not be conformed to the passions of your former ignorance, but as he who called you is holy, you also be holy in all your conduct, since it is written, "You shall be holy, for I am holy."

(Further study: Hebrews 13:20-21)

Being redeemed, we progressively become more Christ-like:
Head: Knowledge, Understanding, Wisdom, Worldview
Heart: Attitude, Emotions, Motives, Feelings, Desires
Hands: Actions, Relationships, Service, Sacrifice

Q98. What means does the Holy Spirit use to mature Christians?

In accordance with His sovereign power, the Holy Spirit uses means such as the Bible, prayer, preaching, discipleship, trials, Christian fellowship and accountability in the process of maturing Christians.

2 Timothy 3:16-17 All Scripture is breathed out by God and profitable for teaching, for reproof, for correction, and for training in righteousness, that the man of God may be complete, equipped for every good work.

1 Thessalonians 5:16-18 ... pray without ceasing ...

2 Timothy 4:2 (NASB) preach the word ...

Matthew 28:18-20 "... make disciples of all nations ..."

Romans 5:3-5 ... we rejoice in our sufferings ...

Hebrews 3:13 ... exhort one another every day ...

(Further study: Acts 2:42; Colossians 3:16)

Bible - Be taught biblically. Read the Bible, hear it, and remember it. Know sound doctrine.

Prayer - Pour out our hearts to God in praise, thanksgiving, confession of sin, and express our requests to Him while submitting to His sovereign will.

Preaching - The word of God taught rightly in the context of a local church.

Discipleship - Follow and learn from more mature Christians and do the work of disciple-making ourselves: call people to saving faith, then train them in sound doctrine and how to live as imitators of Christ.

Trials - Suffer the challenges in life with joy, including overcoming our own sin and other realities of an ungodly world.

Fellowship - Spend quality time with, invite exhortation from, and be accountable to Christians, giving special honor to elders/pastors.

Q99. What are the main identities the Bible gives to the saved?

Our main identities are adopted children, loved slaves, and citizens of the kingdom of God. God moves the saved person from enemy to adopted child, from slave to sin to slave to God, and from alienated to citizen of the kingdom of God.

Ephesians 1:4-5 even as he chose us in him before the foundation of the world, that we should be holy and blameless before him. In love he predestined us for adoption as sons through Jesus Christ, according to the purpose of his will

Romans 8:14 For all who are led by the Spirit of God are sons of God.

Romans 6:20, 22 ... you were slaves of sin ... but now that you have been set free from sin and have become slaves of God, the fruit you get leads to sanctification and its end, eternal life.

Matthew 25:21 (NASB) "His master said to him, 'Well done, good and faithful slave. You were faithful with a few things, I will put you in charge of many things; enter into the joy of your master.'"

Philippians 3:20 But our citizenship is in heaven, and from it we await a Savior, the Lord Jesus Christ

Ephesians 2:19 So then you are no longer strangers and aliens, but you are fellow citizens with the saints and members of the household of God

Hebrews 13:14 For here we have no lasting city, but we seek the city that is to come.

Colossians 1:21 And you, who once were alienated and hostile in mind, doing evil deeds

Romans 5:10 For if while we were enemies we were reconciled to God by the death of his Son, much more, now that we are reconciled, shall we be saved by his life.

Part 10:
Doctrine of the Church
(Ecclesiology)

Word of Truth Catechism

Q100. What is the universal Church?

The universal Church is all the members of the body of Christ, made up of people from all times and around the world. It is all who are called out of darkness, regenerated, and set apart by God's saving grace. It is all the genuine believers in Jesus.

1 Peter 2:9-10 (NASB) But you are a chosen race, a royal priesthood, a holy nation, a people for God's own possession, so that you may proclaim the excellencies of Him who has called you out of darkness into His marvelous light; for you once were not a people, but now you are the people of God; you had not received mercy, but now you have received mercy.

Matthew 16:18 "And I tell you, you are Peter, and on this rock I will build my church, and the gates of hell shall not prevail against it."

Ephesians 5:25 ... Christ loved the church and gave himself up for her

Matthew 28:18-20 And Jesus came and said to them, "All authority in heaven and on earth has been given to me. Go therefore and make disciples of all nations, baptizing them in the name of the Father and of the Son and of the Holy Spirit, teaching them to observe all that I have commanded you. And behold, I am with you always, to the end of the age."

John 10:16 "And I have other sheep that are not of this fold. I must bring them also, and they will listen to my voice. So there will be one flock, one shepherd."

Galatians 3:28 There is neither Jew nor Greek, there is neither slave nor free, there is no male and female, for you are all one in Christ Jesus.

(Further study: Matthew 1:21; John 3:29; Ephesians 4:15-16; Matthew 24:31)

The universal Church is also referred to as the following: the saints, the body of Christ, the bride of Christ, His people, the called-out ones, God's saved elect, and God's saved chosen ones.

Q101. In what way has God commanded the saved to communicate to Him?

We are to communicate to God in persistent prayer.

Romans 12:12 Rejoice in hope, be patient in tribulation, be constant in prayer.

1 Thessalonians 5:16-18 (NASB) Rejoice always; pray without ceasing; in everything give thanks; for this is God's will for you in Christ Jesus.

Colossians 4:2 (NASB) Devote yourselves to prayer, keeping alert in it with an attitude of thanksgiving

1 John 1:9 (NASB) If we confess our sins, He is faithful and righteous to forgive us our sins and to cleanse us from all unrighteousness.

Philippians 4:6 (NASB) Be anxious for nothing, but in everything by prayer and supplication with thanksgiving let your requests be made known to God.

1 Timothy 2:1-2 (NASB) First of all, then, I urge that entreaties and prayers, petitions and thanksgivings, be made on behalf of all men, for kings and all who are in authority, so that we may lead a tranquil and quiet life in all godliness and dignity.

James 4:3 (NASB) You ask and do not receive, because you ask with wrong motives, so that you may spend it on your pleasures.

1 John 5:14-15 (NASB) This is the confidence which we have before Him, that, if we ask anything according to His will, He hears us. And if we know that He hears us in whatever we ask, we know that we have the requests which we have asked from Him.

Hebrews 4:16 (NASB) Therefore let us draw near with confidence to the throne of grace, so that we may receive mercy and find grace to help in time of need.

Matthew 6:9-13 "Pray then like this: Our Father in heaven, hallowed be your name. Your kingdom come, your will be done, on earth as it is in heaven. Give us this day our daily bread, and forgive us our debts, as we also have forgiven our debtors. And lead us not into temptation, but deliver us from evil."

Q102. What is prayer?

Prayer is pouring out our hearts to God in praise, thanksgiving, confession of sin, and expressing our requests to Him while submitting to His sovereign will.

Romans 12:12 Rejoice in hope, be patient in tribulation, be constant in prayer.

1 Thessalonians 5:16-18 (NASB) Rejoice always; pray without ceasing; in everything give thanks; for this is God's will for you in Christ Jesus.

Colossians 4:2 (NASB) Devote yourselves to prayer, keeping alert in it with an attitude of thanksgiving

1 John 1:9 (NASB) If we confess our sins, He is faithful and righteous to forgive us our sins and to cleanse us from all unrighteousness.

Philippians 4:6 (NASB) Be anxious for nothing, but in everything by prayer and supplication with thanksgiving let your requests be made known to God.

James 4:3 (NASB) You ask and do not receive, because you ask with wrong motives, so that you may spend it on your pleasures.

1 John 5:14-15 (NASB) This is the confidence which we have before Him, that, if we ask anything according to His will, He hears us. And if we know that He hears us in whatever we ask, we know that we have the requests which we have asked from Him.

Hebrews 4:16 (NASB) Therefore let us draw near with confidence to the throne of grace, so that we may receive mercy and find grace to help in time of need.

Matthew 6:9-13 "Pray then like this: Our Father in heaven, hallowed be your name. Your kingdom come, your will be done, on earth as it is in heaven. Give us this day our daily bread, and forgive us our debts, as we also have forgiven our debtors. And lead us not into temptation, but deliver us from evil."

(Further study: 1 Timothy 2:1-2)

Q103. How does the Church live in this world?

The Church lives as worshipers of Jesus who make disciples, giving glory to God in all things.

Psalm 105:1-3 (NASB) Oh give thanks to the LORD, call upon His name; Make known His deeds among the peoples. Sing to Him, sing praises to Him; Speak of all His wonders. Glory in His holy name; Let the heart of those who seek the LORD be glad.

Psalm 96:1-5 Oh sing to the LORD a new song; sing to the LORD, all the earth! Sing to the LORD, bless his name; tell of his salvation from day to day. Declare his glory among the nations, his marvelous works among all the peoples! For great is the LORD, and greatly to be praised; he is to be feared above all gods. For all the gods of the peoples are worthless idols, but the LORD made the heavens.

Psalm 96:10 Say among the nations, "The LORD reigns; Indeed, the world is firmly established, it will not be moved; He will judge the peoples with equity."

Matthew 28:18-20 And Jesus came and said to them, "All authority in heaven and on earth has been given to me. Go therefore and make disciples of all nations, baptizing them in the name of the Father and of the Son and of the Holy Spirit, teaching them to observe all that I have commanded you. And behold, I am with you always, to the end of the age."

Romans 11:36 (NASB) For from Him and through Him and to Him are all things. To Him be the glory forever. Amen.

Q104. What is the Great Commission Jesus gave to His Church?

He commissions His Church to be discipled and make disciples among all nations.

Matthew 28:18-20 And Jesus came and said to them, "All authority in heaven and on earth has been given to me. Go therefore and make disciples of all nations, baptizing them in the name of the Father and of the Son and of the Holy Spirit, teaching them to observe all that I have commanded you. And behold, I am with you always, to the end of the age."

Luke 24:47 "... repentance and forgiveness of sins should be proclaimed in his name to all nations, beginning from Jerusalem."

1 John 1:7 (NASB) but if we walk in the Light as He Himself is in the Light, we have fellowship with one another, and the blood of Jesus His Son cleanses us from all sin.

2 Timothy 2:2 (NASB) The things which you have heard from me in the presence of many witnesses, entrust these to faithful men who will be able to teach others also.

Titus 2:3-5 Older women likewise are to be reverent in behavior, not slanderers or slaves to much wine. They are to teach what is good, and so train the young women to love their husbands and children, to be self-controlled, pure, working at home, kind, and submissive to their own husbands, that the word of God may not be reviled.

Ephesians 4:25 Therefore, having put away falsehood, let each one of you speak the truth with his neighbor, for we are members one of another.

Romans 15:14 ... brothers ... you yourselves are full of goodness, filled with all knowledge and able to instruct one another.

Discipleship: The process of following and learning from more mature Christians and doing the work of disciple-making ourselves: calling people to saving faith, then training them in sound doctrine and how to live as imitators of Christ.

Q105. How do we honor the Great Commission?

Based on the Bible, we follow and learn from mature Christians, and we teach others to rightly know and obey Jesus.

2 Timothy 3:16-17 All Scripture is breathed out by God and profitable for teaching, for reproof, for correction, and for training in righteousness, that the man of God may be complete, equipped for every good work.

2 Timothy 2:2 (NASB) The things which you have heard from me in the presence of many witnesses, entrust these to faithful men who will be able to teach others also.

Titus 2:3-5 Older women likewise are to be reverent in behavior, not slanderers or slaves to much wine. They are to teach what is good, and so train the young women to love their husbands and children, to be self-controlled, pure, working at home, kind, and submissive to their own husbands, that the word of God may not be reviled.

2 Timothy 2:24-26 And the Lord's servant must not be quarrelsome but kind to everyone, able to teach, patiently enduring evil, correcting his opponents with gentleness. God may perhaps grant them repentance leading to a knowledge of the truth, and they may come to their senses and escape from the snare of the devil, after being captured by him to do his will.

1 Peter 3:15 but in your hearts honor Christ the Lord as holy, always being prepared to make a defense to anyone who asks you for a reason for the hope that is in you; yet do it with gentleness and respect

Proverbs 1:7 (NASB) The fear of the Lord is the beginning of knowledge; fools despise wisdom and instruction.

Proverbs 15:32 (NASB) He who neglects discipline despises himself, but he who listens to reproof acquires understanding.

(Further study: Ecclesiastes 7:5; Proverbs 27:6; 2 Timothy 4:2; 1 Thessalonians 5:11; Colossians 3:16)

Q106. What is Christian accountability and discipline?

It is loving correction to someone who professes to be a Christian when he/she is out of step of core sound doctrine or practicing other sin. If he/she does not repent after biblical efforts are made, then God's instruction is dis-fellowship until he/she does. All Christians are to joyfully submit to biblically-based accountability.

Hebrews 3:13 But exhort one another every day, as long as it is called "today," that none of you may be hardened by the deceitfulness of sin.

1 Thessalonians 5:14 (NASB) We urge you, brethren, admonish the unruly, encourage the fainthearted, help the weak, be patient with everyone.

1 Corinthians 5:12-13 For what have I to do with judging outsiders? Is it not those inside the church whom you are to judge? God judges those outside. "Purge the evil person from among you."

Hebrews 12:11 For the moment all discipline seems painful rather than pleasant, but later it yields the peaceful fruit of righteousness to those who have been trained by it.

Matthew 18:15-17 (NASB) "If your brother sins, go and show him his fault in private; if he listens to you, you have won your brother. But if he does not listen to you, take one or two more with you, so that BY THE MOUTH OF TWO OR THREE WITNESSES EVERY FACT MAY BE CONFIRMED. If he refuses to listen to them, tell it to the church; and if he refuses to listen even to the church, let him be to you as a Gentile and a tax collector."

(Further study: 2 John 1:9-11; Romans 16:17-18; Galatians 1:8-9; Colossians 3:16; Ephesians 4:2-3; Romans 15:1; Ephesians 5:11; Titus 3:10-11; Galatians 6:1; 2 Thessalonians 3:14-15; Proverbs 15:32; Ecclesiastes 7:5; Proverbs 27:6; Hebrews 3:13; 1 Thessalonians 5:14; 1 Corinthians 5:12-13; Hebrews 12:11; Matthew 18:15-17)

Q107. Why do we do Christian accountability and discipline?

We practice Christian accountability and discipline because of our love for God and our love for one another.

It glorifies God when we trust and obey His commanded will, and it is loving to others to treat them the way God has ordained.

1 John 5:3 (NASB) For this is the love of God, that we keep His commandments; and His commandments are not burdensome.

Galatians 1:10 For am I now seeking the approval of man, or of God? Or am I trying to please man? If I were still trying to please man, I would not be a servant of Christ.

Matthew 18:15 (NASB) "If your brother sins, go and show him his fault in private; if he listens to you, you have won your brother."

1 Corinthians 5:5 you are to deliver this man to Satan for the destruction of the flesh, so that his spirit may be saved in the day of the Lord.

Hebrews 12:11 For the moment all discipline seems painful rather than pleasant, but later it yields the peaceful fruit of righteousness to those who have been trained by it.

Hebrews 3:13 But exhort one another every day, as long as it is called "today," that none of you may be hardened by the deceitfulness of sin.

Proverbs 15:32 (NASB) He who neglects discipline despises himself, but he who listens to reproof acquires understanding.

Ecclesiastes 7:5 (NASB) It is better to listen to the rebuke of a wise man than for one to listen to the song of fools.

Proverbs 27:6 (NASB) Faithful are the wounds of a friend, but deceitful are the kisses of an enemy.

Q108. What is the local church?

The local church is a group of professing believers who have covenanted to unify together to worship and glorify God by fulfilling the commands and mission God has given to the body of Christ.

Hebrews 10:23 Let us hold fast the confession of our hope without wavering, for he who promised is faithful.

1 John 1:7 (NASB) but if we walk in the Light as He Himself is in the Light, we have fellowship with one another, and the blood of Jesus His Son cleanses us from all sin.

Romans 12:3-6 For by the grace given to me I say to everyone among you not to think of himself more highly than he ought to think, but to think with sober judgment, each according to the measure of faith that God has assigned. For as in one body we have many members, and the members do not all have the same function, so we, though many, are one body in Christ, and individually members one of another. Having gifts that differ according to the grace given to us, let us use them ...

1 Corinthians 12:21-26 The eye cannot say to the hand, "I have no need of you," nor again the head to the feet, "I have no need of you." On the contrary, the parts of the body that seem to be weaker are indispensable, and on those parts of the body that we think less honorable we bestow the greater honor, and our unpresentable parts are treated with greater modesty, which our more presentable parts do not require. But God has so composed the body, giving greater honor to the part that lacked it, that there may be no division in the body, but that the members may have the same care for one another. If one member suffers, all suffer together; if one member is honored, all rejoice together.

Ephesians 4:2 with all humility and gentleness, with patience, bearing with one another in love

(Further study: Romans 15:7; 1 Thessalonians 5:11; 1 Peter 1:22-23)

Q109. What are the *primary* duties of the local church?

The local church is to submit to the authority of and diligently teach the Bible, follow the leadership of qualified elders, regularly gather together, serve one another, make disciples, practice higher levels of accountability, and live missional lives together.

1 Timothy 4:13 Until I come, devote yourself to the public reading of Scripture, to exhortation, to teaching.

2 Timothy 3:16-17 All Scripture is breathed out by God and profitable for teaching, for reproof, for correction, and for training in righteousness, that the man of God may be complete, equipped for every good work.

Hebrews 13:17 Obey your leaders and submit to them, for they are keeping watch over your souls, as those who will have to give an account. Let them do this with joy and not with groaning, for that would be of no advantage to you.

Hebrews 10:24-25 And let us consider how to stir up one another to love and good works, not neglecting to meet together, as is the habit of some, but encouraging one another, and all the more as you see the Day drawing near.

Hebrews 3:13 But exhort one another every day, as long as it is called "today," that none of you may be hardened by the deceitfulness of sin.

Colossians 3:16 Let the word of Christ dwell in you richly, teaching and admonishing one another in all wisdom, singing psalms and hymns and spiritual songs, with thankfulness in your hearts to God.

Philippians 2:3 Do nothing from selfish ambition or conceit, but in humility count others more significant than yourselves.

(Further study: Galatians 5:13; Romans 14:19)

Q110. What are the three roles in the local church?

The Bible distinctly instructs a local church to have qualified elders and committed members, of which some may be qualified deacons.

1 Peter 5:1-2 So I exhort the elders among you, as a fellow elder and a witness of the sufferings of Christ, as well as a partaker in the glory that is going to be revealed: shepherd the flock of God that is among you ...

Hebrews 13:17 Obey your leaders and submit to them, for they are keeping watch over your souls, as those who will have to give an account. Let them do this with joy and not with groaning, for that would be of no advantage to you.

Romans 12:3-6 For by the grace given to me I say to everyone among you not to think of himself more highly than he ought to think, but to think with sober judgment, each according to the measure of faith that God has assigned. For as in one body we have many members, and the members do not all have the same function, so we, though many, are one body in Christ, and individually members one of another. Having gifts that differ according to the grace given to us, let us use them ...

Hebrews 10:24-25 And let us consider how to stir up one another to love and good works, not neglecting to meet together, as is the habit of some, but encouraging one another, and all the more as you see the Day drawing near.

(Further study: 1 Timothy 3:1-7; 5:17; Titus 1:5-9; 1 Timothy 3:8-13)

Elders: Qualified and called men who lead, teach, and govern the local church based on the doctrine and authority of Scripture, exercising wisdom in all matters.
Deacons: Qualified and called men who have dedicated, assigned roles of service under the authority of the elders.
Members (Local Church Members): The professing believers who make up the local church family. Church members are committed to Scripture and one another.

Q111. What is baptism?

Baptism is a holy, New Covenant ordinance from our Lord Jesus, whereby a professing believer in Jesus Christ testifies of his/her faith in Christ alone for salvation and his/her union with Christ's death, burial, and resurrection by the public testimony of immersion in water in the name of the Father and of the Son and of the Holy Spirit. Baptism is to be done once and in no way contributes to one's salvation.

Matthew 28:18-20 And Jesus came and said to them, "All authority in heaven and on earth has been given to me. Go therefore and make disciples of all nations, baptizing them in the name of the Father and of the Son and of the Holy Spirit, teaching them to observe all that I have commanded you. And behold, I am with you always, to the end of the age."

Acts 8:12 (NASB) But when they believed Philip preaching the good news about the kingdom of God and the name of Jesus Christ, they were being baptized, men and women alike.

Acts 2:38 (NASB) Peter said to them, "Repent, and each of you be baptized in the name of Jesus Christ ..."

Acts 8:35-38 Then Philip opened his mouth, and beginning with this Scripture he told him the good news about Jesus. And as they were going along the road they came to some water, and the eunuch said, "See, here is water! What prevents me from being baptized?" And he commanded the chariot to stop, and they both went down into the water, Philip and the eunuch, and he baptized him.

Romans 6:3-5 Do you not know that all of us who have been baptized into Christ Jesus were baptized into his death? We were buried therefore with him by baptism into death, in order that, just as Christ was raised from the dead by the glory of the Father, we too might walk in newness of life. For if we have been united with him in a death like his, we shall certainly be united with him in a resurrection like his.

Q112. What is the Lord's Supper?

The Lord's Supper is a holy, New Covenant ordinance from our Lord Jesus, whereby professing believers gather together regularly to remember, celebrate, and testify of the sacrificial death of Jesus Christ by the eating of bread and the drinking of wine, which symbolize the body and blood of Jesus. This is a regular practice and testimony for those who are saved by God.

Matthew 26:26-29 (NASB) While they were eating, Jesus took some bread, and after a blessing, He broke it and gave it to the disciples, and said, "Take, eat; this is My body." And when He had taken a cup and given thanks, He gave it to them, saying, "Drink from it, all of you; for this is My blood of the covenant, which is poured out for many for forgiveness of sins. But I say to you, I will not drink of this fruit of the vine from now on until that day when I drink it new with you in My Father's kingdom."

1 Corinthians 11:23-31 (NASB) For I received from the Lord that which I also delivered to you, that the Lord Jesus in the night in which He was betrayed took bread; and when He had given thanks, He broke it and said, "This is My body, which is for you; do this in remembrance of Me." In the same way He took the cup also after supper, saying, "This cup is the new covenant in My blood; do this, as often as you drink it, in remembrance of Me." For as often as you eat this bread and drink the cup, you proclaim the Lord's death until He comes. Therefore whoever eats the bread or drinks the cup of the Lord in an unworthy manner, shall be guilty of the body and the blood of the Lord. But a man must examine himself, and in so doing he is to eat of the bread and drink of the cup. For he who eats and drinks, eats and drinks judgment to himself if he does not judge the body rightly. For this reason many among you are weak and sick, and a number sleep. But if we judged ourselves rightly, we would not be judged.

(Further study: 2 Corinthians 13:5; 1 Corinthians 10:21)

Q113. What is a spiritual gift?

A spiritual gift is a God-given capacity through which the Holy Spirit supernaturally ministers for the good of the Church unto God's glory.

1 Corinthians 12:4-7 Now there are varieties of gifts, but the same Spirit; and there are varieties of service, but the same Lord; and there are varieties of activities, but it is the same God who empowers them all in everyone. To each is given the manifestation of the Spirit for the common good.

1 Corinthians 12:1-2 Now concerning spiritual gifts, brothers, I do not want you to be uninformed. You know that when you were pagans you were led astray to mute idols, however you were led.

Romans 12:5-9 so we, though many, are one body in Christ, and individually members one of another. Having gifts that differ according to the grace given to us, let us use them: if prophecy, in proportion to our faith; if service, in our serving; the one who teaches, in his teaching; the one who exhorts, in his exhortation; the one who contributes, in generosity; the one who leads, with zeal; the one who does acts of mercy, with cheerfulness. Let love be genuine. Abhor what is evil; hold fast to what is good.

(Further study: 1 Corinthians 12:11; 1 Peter 4:10)

Spiritual Gift: A God-given capacity through which the Holy Spirit supernaturally ministers for the good of the Church unto God's glory. The world tries to counterfeit gifts to confuse, mislead, and cause chaos; therefore, believers must understand what gifts remain, distinguish real gifts, and exercise their gifts in truth. God still does miracles, but the miraculous and revelatory gifts seen in the Old and New Testaments have ceased with the completion of Scripture and the end of the office of Apostles of Christ in the first century. Remaining gifts for the church today include glorious things like service, teaching, exhortation, generosity, leadership, acts of mercy, proclamation of God's truths, and faith.

Q114. Are all the biblical spiritual gifts given still?

No. God used certain gifts for a particular purpose and time in human history. God still does miracles, but the gifts that have ceased to be given by God to individuals are the miraculous and revelatory gifts: Apostle of Christ, prophecy, speaking in tongues, interpreting tongues, and miracle worker.

2 Corinthians 12:12 (NASB) The signs of a true apostle were performed among you with all perseverance, by signs and wonders and miracles.

Ephesians 2:18-22 For through [Jesus] we both have access in one Spirit to the Father. So then you are no longer strangers and aliens, but you are fellow citizens with the saints and members of the household of God, built on the foundation of the apostles and prophets, Christ Jesus himself being the cornerstone, in whom the whole structure, being joined together, grows into a holy temple in the Lord. In him you also are being built together into a dwelling place for God by the Spirit.

Hebrews 1:1-2 Long ago, at many times and in many ways, God spoke to our fathers by the prophets, but in these last days he has spoken to us by his Son, whom he appointed the heir of all things, through whom also he created the world.

Romans 15:4 (NASB) For whatever was written in earlier times was written for our instruction, so that through perseverance and the encouragement of the Scriptures we might have hope.

2 Peter 1:20-21 (NASB) But know this first of all, that no prophecy of Scripture is a matter of one's own interpretation, for no prophecy was ever made by an act of human will, but men moved by the Holy Spirit spoke from God.

Part 11:
Doctrine of the Last Things and Eternity (Eschatology)

Q115. Beyond this life, are there other opportunities to be redeemed from guilt and reconciled to God?

No. Beyond this one life, there are no additional chances to repent and trust in Jesus alone.

Hebrews 9:27 And just as it is appointed for man to die once, and after that comes judgment

2 Corinthians 5:10 For we must all appear before the judgment seat of Christ, so that each one may receive what is due for what he has done in the body, whether good or evil.

Q116. What happens to people when they physically die?

The bodies of those who have died return to dust and decay; however, their souls neither die nor sleep, because they have an immortal character. At death, the souls of the righteous are made perfect in holiness and are received into paradise, where they are with Christ and enjoy God's glory while they wait for the full redemption of their bodies. The souls of the wicked are sent by God to Hades, where they remain in torment and utter darkness awaiting the final judgment.

Genesis 3:19 "By the sweat of your face you shall eat bread, till you return to the ground, for out of it you were taken; for you are dust, and to dust you shall return."

Ecclesiastes 12:7 and the dust returns to the earth as it was, and the spirit returns to God who gave it.

2 Corinthians 5:8 Yes, we are of good courage, and we would rather be away from the body and at home with the Lord.

Luke 23:43 And he said to him, "Truly, I say to you, today you will be with me in paradise."

Philippians 1:23 I am hard pressed between the two. My desire is to depart and be with Christ, for that is far better.

1 Corinthians 15:51-53 (NASB) Behold, I tell you a mystery; we will not all sleep, but we will all be changed, in a moment, in the twinkling of an eye, at the last trumpet; for the trumpet will sound, and the dead will be raised imperishable, and we will be changed. For this perishable must put on the imperishable, and this mortal [body] must put on immortality.

Luke 16:22-23 "... The rich man also died and was buried, and in Hades, being in torment ..."

Q117. What is the final judgment?

God has appointed a day in which He will righteously judge the world by Jesus Christ, in Whom is all power and judgment. On that day, the fallen angels and all people who were conceived to life will appear before the judgment seat of Christ to give an account of all their thoughts, words, and deeds — whether good or evil. God's purpose for this day is for the manifestation of the glory, both of His merciful grace in the eternal salvation of the elect and of His justice in the eternal damnation of the reprobate.

Acts 17:31 "because he has fixed a day on which he will judge the world in righteousness by a man whom he has appointed; and of this he has given assurance to all by raising him from the dead."

John 5:27 "And he [the Father] has given him [Jesus] authority to execute judgment, because he is the Son of Man."

2 Corinthians 5:10 For we must all appear before the judgment seat of Christ, so that each one may receive what is due for what he has done in the body, whether good or evil.

Matthew 25:31-32 "... [Jesus] will sit on his glorious throne. Before him will be gathered all the nations, and he will separate people one from another one from another as a shepherd separates the sheep from the goats."

Romans 9:22-24 What if God, desiring to show his wrath and to make known his power, has endured with much patience vessels of wrath prepared for destruction, in order to make known the riches of his glory for vessels of mercy, which he has prepared beforehand for glory — even us whom he has called, not from the Jews only but also from the Gentiles?

(Further study: Ecclesiastes 12:14; Romans 14:10-12; Matthew 12:36; Jude 6; Revelation 20:15; Matthew 25:31-34, 41, 46)

Q118. At the final judgment, what happens to people who did not have saving faith in Christ Jesus?

Their souls will be united forever with their bodies, and upon their final judgment, they will be thrown into hell and punished by God's wrath forever because of their guilt.

Acts 24:15 (NASB) "... there shall certainly be a resurrection of both the righteous and the wicked."

John 5:28-29 "Do not marvel at this, for an hour is coming when all who are in the tombs will hear his voice and come out, those who have done good to the resurrection of life, and those who have done evil to the resurrection of judgment."

Revelation 20:15 (NASB) And if anyone's name was not found written in the book of life, he was thrown into the lake of fire.

Matthew 25:46 (NASB) "These [all unbelievers] will go away into eternal punishment ..."

Luke 12:5 (NASB) "But I will warn you whom to fear: fear the One who, after He has killed, has authority to cast into hell; yes, I tell you, fear Him!"

1 Corinthians 15:22 (NASB) For as in Adam all die ...

1 Corinthians 6:9-10 Or do you not know that the unrighteous will not inherit the kingdom of God? Do not be deceived: neither the sexually immoral, nor idolaters, nor adulterers, nor men who practice homosexuality, nor thieves, nor the greedy, nor drunkards, nor revilers, nor swindlers will inherit the kingdom of God.

Romans 2:8 ... for those who are self-seeking and do not obey the truth, but obey unrighteousness, there will be wrath and fury.

John 3:18 "... whoever does not believe is condemned already, because he has not believed in the name of the only Son of God."

2 Thessalonians 2:12 ... all may be condemned who did not believe the truth but had pleasure in unrighteousness.

Q119. What is hell?

Hell is the place of eternal death with dreadful and endless torment. The worst part of hell is not getting to enjoy the blessed presence of and reconciliation to God. In hell, God is rightly punishing both humans who did not repent and trust in Jesus and fallen angels.

Matthew 25:46 (NASB) "These [all unbelievers] will go away into eternal punishment ..."

2 Thessalonians 1:7-9 ... when the Lord Jesus is revealed from heaven with his mighty angels in flaming fire, inflicting vengeance on those who do not know God and on those who do not obey the gospel of our Lord Jesus. They will suffer the punishment of eternal destruction, away from the presence of the Lord and from the glory of his might

Revelation 14:10-11 "he [the unbeliever] also will drink the wine of God's wrath, poured full strength into the cup of his anger, and he will be tormented with fire and sulfur in the presence of the holy angels and in the presence of the Lamb. And the smoke of their torment goes up forever and ever, and they have no rest, day or night ..."

Matthew 8:12 (NASB) "... outer darkness; in that place there will be weeping and gnashing of teeth."

Revelation 20:10 (NASB) And the devil who deceived them was thrown into the lake of fire and brimstone, where the beast and the false prophet are also; and they will be tormented day and night forever and ever.

Mark 9:43 "And if your hand causes you to sin, cut it off. It is better for you to enter life crippled than with two hands to go to hell, to the unquenchable fire."

Mark 9:47-48 "... It is better for you to enter the kingdom of God with one eye than with two eyes to be thrown into hell, 'where their worm does not die and the fire is not quenched.'"

Q120. At the final judgment, what happens to people who had saving faith in Christ Jesus?

Their souls will be united forever with their bodies, now finally glorified, and upon their final judgment, these people will go into everlasting life and receive fullness of joy and glory with everlasting rewards in the blessed presence of the Lord.

1 Corinthians 15:51-52 (NASB) Behold, I tell you a mystery; we will not all sleep, but we will all be changed, in a moment, in the twinkling of an eye, at the last trumpet ...

Acts 24:15 (NASB) "having a hope in God, which these men cherish themselves, that there shall certainly be a resurrection of both the righteous and the wicked."

John 14:6 Jesus said to him, "I am the way, and the truth, and the life. No one comes to the Father except through me."

Ephesians 2:8-9 For by grace you have been saved through faith. And this is not your own doing; it is the gift of God, not a result of works, so that no one may boast.

Revelation 21:27 But nothing unclean will ever enter it [the new creation], nor anyone who does what is detestable or false, but only those who are written in the Lamb's book of life.

2 Corinthians 5:10 For we must all appear before the judgment seat of Christ, so that each one may receive what is due for what he has done in the body, whether good or evil.

Matthew 25:21 (NASB) "His master said to him, 'Well done, good and faithful slave. You were faithful with a few things, I will put you in charge of many things; enter into the joy of your master.'"

Matthew 25:34 (NASB) "Then the King will say to those on His right, 'Come, you who are blessed of My Father, inherit the kingdom prepared for you from the foundation of the world.'"

Matthew 25:46 (NASB) "... the righteous [will go] into eternal life."

Q121. What is our final glorification?

Final glorification is the future work of God upon Christians when those souls who haven't been fully changed yet are made perfect in holiness, and He transforms all the mortal, physical bodies of the saved to eternal, glorified physical bodies in which we will dwell forever in the new heaven and the new earth.

1 Corinthians 15:49 Just as we have borne the image of the man of dust, we shall also bear the image of the man of heaven.

Philippians 3:20-21 But our citizenship is in heaven, and from it we await a Savior, the Lord Jesus Christ, who will transform our lowly body to be like his glorious body, by the power that enables him even to subject all things to himself.

1 Corinthians 15:51-53 (NASB) Behold, I tell you a mystery; we will not all sleep, but we will all be changed, in a moment, in the twinkling of an eye, at the last trumpet; for the trumpet will sound, and the dead will be raised imperishable, and we will be changed. For this perishable must put on the imperishable, and this mortal [body] must put on immortality.

1 John 3:2 (NASB) Beloved, now we are children of God, and it has not appeared as yet what we will be. We know that when He appears, we will be like Him, because we will see Him just as He is.

Q122. What will eternal life be like in the new heaven and new earth for the elect?

Eternal life will be a more intimate communion with God, and we will be free from sin, evil, sickness, suffering, and death. We will be in the Lord's presence, glorifying Him for all eternity. It is better than we can even imagine.

Matthew 25:34 (NASB) "Then the King will say to those on His right, 'Come, you who are blessed of My Father, inherit the kingdom prepared for you from the foundation of the world.'"

Matthew 25:46 (NASB) "... the righteous [will go] into eternal life."

Revelation 21:4 "He will wipe away every tear from their eyes, and death shall be no more, neither shall there be mourning, nor crying, nor pain anymore, for the former things have passed away."

1 Corinthians 2:9 But, as it is written, "What no eye has seen, nor ear heard, nor the heart of man imagined, what God has prepared for those who love him"

2 Corinthians 4:17 For this light momentary affliction is preparing for us an eternal weight of glory beyond all comparison

Romans 8:18 For I consider that the sufferings of this present time are not worth comparing with the glory that is to be revealed to us.

Revelation 7:9-10 After this I looked, and behold, a great multitude that no one could number, from every nation, from all tribes and peoples and languages, standing before the throne and before the Lamb, clothed in white robes, with palm branches in their hands, and crying out with a loud voice, "Salvation belongs to our God who sits on the throne, and to the Lamb!"

2 Timothy 4:8 (NASB) in the future there is laid up for me the crown of righteousness, which the Lord, the righteous Judge, will award to me on that day; and not only to me, but also to all who have loved His appearing.

Appendix I:
Glossary

Adamic Covenant (The Covenant of Works): The covenant required that Adam obey and trust God entirely. In this, obedience would be rewarded with eternal life and blessing, but disobedience would be punished with curse and death. Adam disobeyed, bringing the consequences upon mankind.

Adoption: The gracious act of God in which He makes a believer one of His children, giving the privileges of sonship.

Angels: Created spiritual beings who have limited power and are under God's control.

Anthropomorphic: Ascribing a human body, appearance, functions, or parts to something that is not human.

Anthropopathic: Ascribing human feelings/passions to something that is not human.

Aseity *(As God's attribute):* God does not owe His existence to anything or anyone outside Himself, nor does He need anything beyond Himself to maintain His existence. He is self-contained, self-existent, self-sufficient, and independent (Psalm 90:2; Psalm 102:24–27; John 5:26; Hebrews 13:8; Revelation 1:8).

Authority of Scripture: As God's word, the Bible is our rule; it is always the final and authoritative word.

Baptism: A holy, New Covenant ordinance from our Lord Jesus, whereby a professing believer in Jesus Christ testifies of his/her faith in Christ alone for salvation and his/her union with Christ's death, burial, and resurrection by the public testimony of immersion in water in the name of the Father and of the Son and of the Holy Spirit. Baptism is to be done once and in no way contributes to one's salvation.

Call (See *General Gospel Call* and *Effectual Call*)

Church (See *Universal Church* and *Local church*)

Conversion: As a result of regeneration, God immediately gives the gift of saving faith by which a person willingly repents of sin and trusts his/her life and salvation to Jesus Christ alone.

Covenant of Redemption: The Covenant of Redemption is the plan and decree made before creation between God the Father, God the Son, and God the Holy Spirit to graciously redeem the chosen ones from sin and punishment based on the work required of Jesus. All of creation is set in the context of this divine plan.

Deacons: Qualified and called men who have dedicated, assigned roles of service under the authority of the elders.

Didactic: Instructive; teaching a fact of truth in a clear, direct method.

Discipleship: The process of following and learning from more mature Christians and doing the work of disciple-making ourselves: calling people to saving faith, then training them in sound doctrine and how to live as imitators of Christ.

Disobedience in Heart: Having the wrong state of mind, motivation, or desires behind what we do or feel.

Disobedience in Deed: Doing or saying what God forbids, or not doing or saying what God commands.

Divine Covenant: A relational agreement initiated by God that may include obligations, rewards, and/or punishments from Him.

Effective Call (Irresistible Grace): The act of God in which He graciously summons each of the elect to Himself, regenerates them, and gives saving faith, so they willingly respond with genuine repentance and trust in Jesus Christ. God's effective call — saving grace — always brings about the response it demands in people's hearts.

Elders: Qualified and called men who lead, teach, and govern the local church based on the doctrine and authority of Scripture, exercising wisdom in all matters.

Election (See *Unconditional Individual Election*)

Eternal and Infinite (*As God's attribute):* God is timeless, having always existed, and without measure or limit in greatness or duration. He transcends time and has no beginning and no end. God is infinite in essence — absolutely perfect. There are no constraints upon Him from outside of Himself (Deuteronomy 33:27; Isaiah 40:28; Psalm 90:2; Psalms 147:5; Psalms 145:3).

Expiation: Jesus takes away the guilt of the elect based on His substitutionary atonement.

Fear of God: The terror of judgment and wrath for unbelievers; the right awe, humbleness, and respect for God that flows from the hearts of all believers.

Federal Headship of Adam: God chose Adam as the Federal Head (representative) of all mankind. Because Adam failed to obey God's commands perfectly, all those he represented receive the results of his disobedience. Given God's perfect wisdom, we can never argue that Adam was a poor choice to represent us. God's choice of Adam as the first Federal Head was an infallible (perfect) choice; Adam represented us accurately. If we are to be reconciled to God, we need a second and final Federal Head to redeem and represent us. For the salvation of the elect, God ordained Jesus as the second and final Federal Head.

Final Glorification: The future work of God upon Christians when those souls who haven't been fully changed yet are made perfect in holiness, and He transforms all the mortal, physical bodies of the saved to eternal, glorified physical bodies in which we will dwell forever in the new heaven and the new earth.

Foreknowledge: God knows all things eternally and has decreed in Himself, from all eternity, by the most wise and holy counsel of His own will, freely and unchangeably, all things, whatsoever comes to pass; therefore, He knows what will come to pass *in time*. However, the words "foreknowledge" and "foreknew" are never used in the New Testament in connection with human actions; instead, they always have reference to persons. These passages are speaking about God's choice of the elect for saving grace. Through Christ before the creation of the world, God chose His elect in love (Romans 8:29-30; Acts 2:23; 1 Peter 1:1-2; 1 Peter 1:19-20; Matthew 7:21-23).

General Gospel Call: The gospel of Jesus Christ being proclaimed to all tribes, tongues, and nations. God has ordained that gospel proclamation is the vehicle by which He sets the table for salvation.

Glorification (See *Final Glorification*)

Glory of God: God's holiness, infinite beauty, and the greatness of His limitless perfection shining out to all of creation.

Goodness (*As God's attribute*): All that God is and does is perfectly good, and He alone is the final standard of good. There is such an absolute perfection in God's nature and being that nothing is lacking or defective in Him, and nothing can be added to make Him better (Psalm 34:8; Psalm 145:9; Psalm 25:8; Matthew 7:7-11; Romans 8:28-29).

Grace (*As God's attribute*): Grace is a perfection of the divine character, which is exercised only toward the elect. Grace is distinguished from "mercy." God gives unmerited grace to the guilty and unworthy that He has chosen. This includes blessings such as regeneration, faith, reconciliation, sanctification, and eternal life (Ephesians 1:2-14; Romans 11:6; Romans 3:10-12; Ephesians 2:8-9; Hebrews 4:16).

Grace: Unmerited favor (or an undeserved gift) given by an unobligated giver.

Hell: The place of eternal death with dreadful and endless torment. The worst part of hell is not getting to enjoy the blessed presence of and reconciliation to God. In hell, God is rightly punishing both humans who did not repent and trust in Jesus and fallen angels.

Holiness *(As God's attribute):* God is distinct, separate, and in a class by Himself (set apart). He is superior to creation in every way and above all. He is morally pure (without any sin), and He is holy in relation to every aspect of His nature and character. Purity and the sum of all moral excellency are found in Him (Exodus 15:11; 1 Samuel 2:2; Revelation 4:8; 1 Peter 1:14-16; 1 John 1:5; Psalm 99:3).

Human Inability: In and of oneself, a person can do nothing that honors God and has no will that longs to trust in Jesus. After Adam, all of mankind are born spiritually dead sinners; each person continues in sin, is unable to do anything that genuinely seeks for or glorifies God, and deserves only God's righteous wrath. (Also see *Total Depravity*)

Humiliation of Christ: Jesus, in obedience to God the Father, took on human nature, came under the law, was tempted in this life, suffered the wrath of God by being cursed on the cross, and died a physical death.

Hypostatic Union: Jesus Christ's eternal, fully divine nature being united to His fully human nature at His incarnation. These two natures are not mixed, confused, or changed but are united without loss of separate identity, and they are inseparable.

Immutability *(As God's attribute):* God, in His being, perfections, will, purposes, ordinations, and promises, does not change in any way. He has always been and will always be exactly the same (Numbers 23:19-20; James 1:17; 1 Samuel 15:29; Exodus 3:14; Acts 14:15).

Impassibility *(As God's attribute):* God does not experience emotional changes either from within or effected by His relationship to creation. He remains unchanged and unchanging, both prior and subsequent to creation (Numbers 23:19-20; Malachi 3:6; James 1:17; 1 Samuel 15:29; Exodus 3:14).

Imputation: When something not of your own is credited (accounted) to you. Adam's guilt was imputed to all persons. The sin of the elect was imputed to Jesus at the cross, and Jesus' perfect righteousness is imputed to the elect at conversion.

Inability (See *Human Inability* and *Total Depravity*)

Inerrancy of Scripture (Inerrant): The Bible, in the original manuscripts, is without error in all its teaching; it does not affirm anything that is contrary to fact. The Bible is a reflection of its perfect Author.

Infallibility of Scripture (Infallible): The Bible never fails. It is completely trustworthy as the sole objective source of all God has given us about Himself, His plan for humanity, and the life of faith. The Bible will not fail to accomplish its purpose.

Irresistible Grace: (See *Effective Call*)

Justice *(As God's attribute):* Based on God's own perfect righteousness and holiness, He deals with all things rightly and completely. All that God has decreed and all that He does is completely just. He hates sin and always judges perfectly (Job 34:12; Deuteronomy 32:4; Psalms 9:7-8; Romans 12:19; Romans 3:26).

Justification: God declares a believer *not guilty* based on the believer being credited Jesus Christ's perfect righteousness.

Law (See *Positive Law*, *Threefold Use of the Universal Moral Law*, and *Universal Moral Law [Natural Law]*)

Limited Atonement (also known as Definite Atonement and Particular Atonement): Christ's work on the cross was not done for every human to ever live; rather, it was done exclusively for God's elect, who are chosen people from throughout all of human history and represent every tribe, tongue, and nation. In doing this, Christ accomplished substitutionary atonement for the chosen ones by cancelling the debt of all their sin, appeasing God's holy wrath, and earning all the benefits of their salvation.

Local Church: A group of professing believers who have covenanted to unify together to worship and glorify God by fulfilling the commands and mission God has given to the body of Christ.

Lord's Supper: A holy, New Covenant ordinance from our Lord Jesus, whereby professing believers gather together regularly to remember, celebrate, and testify of the sacrificial death of Jesus Christ in place of His chosen ones by the eating of bread and the drinking of wine, which symbolize the body and blood of Jesus. This is a regular practice and testimony for those who are saved by God.

Love *(As God's attribute):* God is love; it is not simply that God loves, but that He is love itself, and any true love has its origin in Him. God gives Himself for the blessing and salvation of undeserving sinners. The love of God is uninfluenced; there was nothing in the recipients of His love to call it into exercise, and nothing in the recipients to attract or prompt it (1 John 4:8; Ephesians 5:1-2; John 15:9-11; Romans 5:8; Ephesians 1:2-6).

Members (Local Church Members): The professing believers who make up the local church family. Church members are committed to Scripture and one another.

Necessity of Scripture: We need the Bible; we cannot rightly know God or what He requires of man without the special revelation of the Bible.

New Covenant (The Covenant of Grace): The covenant by which God saves the elect, by grace through faith in Jesus Christ. The New Covenant was planned before creation, promised in Genesis after the fall, and formally established by the blood of Christ when the work required of Him was complete.

Old Covenant: The Old Covenant was a temporary covenant made primarily with Israelites and was defined by the Abrahamic Covenant, conditioned by the Mosaic Covenant, and focused by the Davidic Covenant. This covenant offered temporary blessings but did not offer eternal life. Through promises, types, and shadows it taught about the Messiah, who was to come to fulfill the law, establish the New Covenant, and redeem the elect.

Omnipotence *(As God's attribute):* God is able to do all His holy will. He is all-powerful (Psalm 33:9; Isaiah 46:10; Jeremiah 32:17; Matthew 19:26; Job 42:2).

Omnipresence *(As God's attribute):* God does not have size or spatial dimensions and is present at every point of space with His whole being. Nothing in the universe exists outside the presence of God (Psalm 139:7-10; Jeremiah 23:24; Deuteronomy 4:39; Hebrews 13:5; Revelation 14:10).

Omniscience *(As God's attribute):* God has perfect, complete knowledge. He knows all things that exist and all things that could have existed. He never learns, nor does He forget. God cannot grow in understanding, knowledge, or wisdom, because He lacks nothing (Job 37:16; Psalm 147:5; Isaiah 46:9-10; Romans 11:33-34; Matthew 11:21, 23).

Original Sin: The inherited guilt and corruption of man's nature as a direct result of Adam's sin. Because of God's system of headship, when Adam sinned, in some sense, all of mankind sinned with him; therefore, Adam's guilt is every person's guilt. In addition to the legal guilt that God imputes to each person, everyone also inherits a sinful nature and the other consequences brought on because of Adam's sin.

Perseverance of the Saints: God keeps His saved people forever. The elect are saved and eternally secure by God's power and promise. Because of grace, God works so those whom He has chosen and given eternal salvation, by the power and work of the Holy Spirit, are enabled to persevere in faith forever. A person shows that he/she was truly saved by God by persevering in faith in Christ until the end.

Positive Law: Law and commands based on the will of God for a particular people, a particular purpose, and a particular time.

Prayer: Pouring out our hearts to God in praise, thanksgiving, confession of sin, and expressing our requests to Him while submitting to His sovereign will.

Predestination: In love, based on the perfect will of the Triune God, the destiny of salvation unto eternal life for God's chosen people was planned and ordained from start to end before creation began. Predestination is not based on foreseen deeds or faith in anyone; it is based on God's will alone.

Progressive Sanctification: Growing in holiness through obedience to the Lordship of Jesus and His word from a right heart. By grace, it is a lifelong process powered by the Holy Spirit to change believers to become more like Christ.

Propitiation: Jesus satisfies God's wrath due the elect based on His substitutionary atonement.

Regeneration (New Birth, Becoming Born Again): The act by which God, by His power and will, gives new life to the spiritually dead. Regeneration immediately precedes the gift of saving faith.

Saving Faith: Rather than trusting one's own assumed worth, works, or ability, a person repents and believes that Jesus is God, trusts in Jesus' sinless life of perfect obedience, Jesus' sacrificial death on the cross in his/her place, and Jesus' rising from the dead to claim salvation and victory for him/her. Saving faith is produced in the elect by God and is always accompanied by progressive sanctification and ongoing repentance from sin.

Sovereignty *(As God's attribute)*: As the one true Ruler and Owner of creation, God has rightful and complete authority over all things. He has legitimate claim to absolute lordship, and His governing is just. Providentially, God controls and directs all things, and He does so to fulfill His purposes after the counsel of His own holy will for His glory. God is the Supreme Being who answers to no one and who has the absolute right to do with His creation as He desires; nothing happens without His ordination (Psalm 115:3; Ephesians 1:11; Daniel 4:35; Psalm 139:16; Isaiah 45:7).

Spiritual Gift: A God-given capacity through which the Holy Spirit supernaturally ministers for the good of the Church unto God's glory. The world tries to counterfeit gifts to confuse, mislead, and cause chaos; therefore, believers must understand what gifts remain, distinguish real gifts, and exercise their gifts in truth. God still does miracles, but the miraculous and revelatory gifts seen in the Old and New Testaments have ceased with the completion of Scripture and the end of the office of Apostles of Christ in the first century. Remaining gifts for the church today include glorious things like service, teaching, exhortation, generosity, leadership, acts of mercy, proclamation of God's truths, and faith.

Spirituality *(As God's attribute):* God is spirit. He exists as a being that has no parts or dimensions, is not made of any matter, and is more excellent than any other kind of existence. He is an invisible, immaterial, and infinite being that is fundamentally distinct from visible, material, and finite creatures (John 4:24; 1 Timothy 1:17; Matthew 1:23; Colossians 1:15; Luke 24:39).

Substitutionary Atonement: On the cross, Christ fully satisfied God's divine wrath as the perfect substitute in place of His elect.

Sufficiency of Scripture: The Bible is enough; it tells us who God is, who man is in relation to Him, what God has done, and what God requires of man.

Threefold Use of the Universal Moral Law:
>**First Function**: It reveals both the perfect righteousness of God and man's own sinfulness and shortcomings.
>**Second Function**: It aids in restraining evil throughout mankind. To some degree, it secures civil order and keeps mankind from practicing even more sin than what is done.
>**Third Function**: It informs the saved of the good works that God has planned for them; it aids them to learn in truth with greater confidence what the will of the Lord is.

Total Depravity: As a result of Adam's sin, every person born of both man and woman has inherited a sin nature and is utterly dependent on saving grace exerted by God for a new nature and salvation. Because of the fall, every part of natural man has been corrupted by sin: his mind, will, emotions, and flesh. Sin affects the whole person; all people sin because they are sinners by nature. All men are conceived in sin, dead in sin, slaves to sin, and deserving of God's wrath. Total depravity does not mean that man is without a conscience or any sense of right or wrong, nor does it mean that man is as wicked or sinful as he could be. Total depravity recognizes the Bible teaches that even the apparent "good" things unregenerate man does are ruined by sin, because they are not done out of faith in Jesus for the glory of God. (Also see *Human Inability*)

Trinity: One God, three Persons. There is but one eternal Godhead that exists in three co-equal, co-eternal Persons: God the Father, God the Son, and God the Holy Spirit. Each Person is fully and completely God; each has the same essence and is described in Scripture as possessing the attributes of God.

Truthfulness and Faithfulness *(As God's attributes)*: God is the original truth, the source of all truth, and the truth in all truth. All that proceeds from Him—all His words, ordinances, paths, works, commandments, and laws—are pure truth. God does not lie. He is faithful and without deceit. All His knowledge and words are both true and the final standard of truth. He keeps all His promises (Isaiah 40:8; Numbers 23:19; John 14:6; John 17:17-19; 2 Timothy 2:15).

Unconditional Individual Election: Before creation existed, God chose which individual human beings would receive salvation from sin, death, and God's eternal wrath. This choice to redeem certain ones is not based on any so-called goodness, will, or work in them; rather, it is based on the freedom and grace of God in Christ Jesus alone.

Universal Church: All the members of the body of Christ, made up of people from all times and around the world. It is all who are called out of darkness, regenerated, and set apart by God's saving grace. It is all the genuine believers in Jesus. The universal Church can be referred to as: the saints, the body of Christ, the bride of Christ, His people, the called-out ones, God's saved elect, and

God's saved chosen ones.

Universal Moral Law (Natural Law): Unchanging law and commands based on the right and character of God, to which man is held accountable for all of life. Universal Moral Law is written in the hearts of all people, leaving them without excuse in disobedience.

Wisdom *(As God's attribute):* God is eternally wise and the source of all wisdom. God possesses wisdom perfectly and has decidedly ordained all things perfectly, including the best ways to accomplish His decisions. The wisdom of God is manifest in His creating, ordering, providence in, and governing of all things (Job 12:13; Isaiah 55:9; Romans 11:33; Romans 11:36; Acts 2:23).

Wrath *(As God's attribute):* God is a God of wrath. The wrath of God is His eternal detestation of all unrighteousness. God has justice against all evil and decreed eternal punishment against unredeemed sinners (Romans 1:18; Psalm 5:5-6; Psalm 11:5; Psalm 7:11; Revelation 14:9-10).

Appendix II:
The 1689 Confession of Faith

Chapter 1: Of The Holy Scriptures

1. The Holy Scripture is the only sufficient, certain, and infallible rule of all saving knowledge, faith, and obedience, although the light of nature, and the works of creation and providence do so far manifest the goodness, wisdom, and power of God, as to leave men inexcusable; yet are they not sufficient to give that knowledge of God and his will which is necessary unto salvation. Therefore it pleased the Lord at sundry times and in divers manners to reveal himself, and to declare that his will unto his church; and afterward for the better preserving and propagating of the truth, and for the more sure establishment and comfort of the church against the corruption of the flesh, and the malice of Satan, and of the world, to commit the same wholly unto writing; which maketh the Holy Scriptures to be most necessary, those former ways of God's revealing his will unto his people being now ceased. (2 Timothy 3:15-17; Isaiah 8:20; Luke 16:29, 31; Ephesians 2:20; Romans 1:19-21; Romans 2:14, 15; Psalms 19:1-3; Hebrews 1:1; Proverbs 22:19-21; Romans 15:4; 2 Peter 1:19, 20)

2. Under the name of Holy Scripture, or the Word of God written, are now contained all the books of the Old and New Testaments, which are these:

Of the Old Testament: Genesis, Exodus, Leviticus, Numbers, Deuteronomy, Joshua, Judges, Ruth, I Samuel, II Samuel, I Kings, II Kings, I Chronicles, II Chronicles, Ezra, Nehemiah, Esther, Job, Psalms, Proverbs, Ecclesiastes, The Song of Solomen, Isaiah, Jeremiah, Lamentations, Ezekiel, Daniel, Hosea, Joel, Amos, Obadiah, Jonah, Micah, Nahum, Habakkuk, Zephaniah, Haggai, Zechariah, Malachi

Of the New Testament: Matthew, Mark, Luke, John, The Acts of the Apostles, Paul's Epistle to the Romans, I Corinthians, II Corinthians, Galatians, Ephesians, Philippians, Colossians, I Thessalonians, II Thessalonians, I Timothy, II Timothy, To Titus, To Philemon, The Epistle to the Hebrews, Epistle of James, The first and second Epistles of Peter, The first, second, and third Epistles of John, The Epistle of Jude, The Revelation

All of which are given by the inspiration of God, to be the rule of faith and life. (2 Timothy 3:16)

3. The books commonly called Apocrypha, not being of divine inspiration, are no part of the canon or rule of the Scripture, and, therefore, are of no authority to the church of God, nor to be any otherwise approved or made use of than other human writings. (Luke 24:27, 44; Romans 3:2)

4. The authority of the Holy Scripture, for which it ought to be believed, dependeth not upon the testimony of any man or church, but wholly upon God (who is truth itself), the author thereof; therefore it is to be received because it is the Word of God. (2 Peter 1:19-21; 2 Timothy 3:16; 2 Thessalonians 2:13; 1 John 5:9)

5. We may be moved and induced by the testimony of the church of God to an high and reverent esteem of the Holy Scriptures; and the heavenliness of the matter, the efficacy of the doctrine, and the majesty of the style, the consent of all the parts, the scope of the whole (which is to give all glory to God), the full discovery it makes of the only way of man's salvation, and many other incomparable excellencies, and entire perfections thereof, are arguments whereby it doth abundantly evidence itself to be the Word of God; yet notwithstanding, our full persuasion and assurance of the infallible truth, and divine authority thereof, is from the inward work of the Holy Spirit bearing witness by and with the Word in our hearts. (John 16:13, 14; 1 Corinthians 2:10-12; 1 John 2:20, 27)

6. The whole counsel of God concerning all things necessary for his own glory, man's salvation, faith and life, is either expressly set down or necessarily contained in the Holy Scripture: unto which nothing at any time is to be added, whether by new revelation of the Spirit, or traditions of men. Nevertheless, we acknowledge the inward illumination of the Spirit of God to be necessary for the saving understanding of such things as are revealed in the Word, and that there are some circumstances concerning the worship of God, and government of the church, common to human actions and societies, which are to be ordered by the light of nature and Christian prudence, according to the general rules of the Word, which are always to be observed. (2 Timothy 3:15-17; Galatians 1:8, 9; John 6:45; 1 Corinthians 2:9-12; 1 Corinthians 11:13, 14; 1 Corinthians 14:26, 40)

7. All things in Scripture are not alike plain in themselves, nor alike clear unto all; yet those things which are necessary to be known, believed and observed for salvation, are so clearly propounded and opened in some place of Scripture or other, that not only the learned, but the unlearned, in a due use of ordinary means, may attain to a sufficient understanding of them. (2 Peter 3:16; Psalms 19:7; Psalms 119:130)

8. The Old Testament in Hebrew (which was the native language of the people of God of old), and the New Testament in Greek (which at the time of the writing of it was most generally known to the nations), being immediately inspired by God, and by his singular care and providence kept pure in all ages, are therefore authentic; so as in all controversies of religion, the church is finally to appeal to them. But because these original tongues are not known to all the people of God, who have a right unto, and interest in the Scriptures, and are commanded in the fear of God to read and search them, therefore they are to be translated into the vulgar language of every nation unto which they come, that the Word of God dwelling plentifully in all, they may worship him in an acceptable manner,

and through patience and comfort of the Scriptures may have hope. (Romans 3:2; Isaiah 8:20; Acts 15:15; John 5:39; 1 Corinthians 14:6, 9, 11, 12, 24, 28; Colossians 3:16)

9. The infallible rule of interpretation of Scripture is the Scripture itself; and therefore when there is a question about the true and full sense of any Scripture (which is not manifold, but one), it must be searched by other places that speak more clearly. (2 Peter 1:20, 21; Acts 15:15, 16)

10. The supreme judge, by which all controversies of religion are to be determined, and all decrees of councils, opinions of ancient writers, doctrines of men, and private spirits, are to be examined, and in whose sentence we are to rest, can be no other but the Holy Scripture delivered by the Spirit, into which Scripture so delivered, our faith is finally resolved. (Matthew 22:29, 31, 32; Ephesians 2:20; Acts 28:23)

Chapter 2: Of God and of the Holy Trinity

1. The Lord our God is but one only living and true God; whose subsistence is in and of himself, infinite in being and perfection; whose essence cannot be comprehended by any but himself; a most pure spirit, invisible, without body, parts, or passions, who only hath immortality, dwelling in the light which no man can approach unto; who is immutable, immense, eternal, incomprehensible, almighty, every way infinite, most holy, most wise, most free, most absolute; working all things according to the counsel of his own immutable and most righteous will for his own glory; most loving, gracious, merciful, long-suffering, abundant in goodness and truth, forgiving iniquity, transgression, and sin; the rewarder of them that diligently seek him, and withal most just and terrible in his judgments, hating all sin, and who will by no means clear the guilty. (1 Corinthians 8:4, 6; Deuteronomy 6:4; Jeremiah 10:10; Isaiah 48:12; Exodus 3:14; John 4:24; 1 Timothy 1:17; Deuteronomy 4:15, 16;

Malachi 3:6; 1 Kings 8:27; Jeremiah 23:23; Psalms 90:2; Genesis 17:1; Isaiah 6:3; Psalms 115:3; Isaiah 46:10; Proverbs 16:4; Romans 11:36; Exodus 34:6, 7; Hebrews 11:6; Nehemiah 9:32, 33; Psalms 5:5, 6; Exodus 34:7; Nahum 1:2, 3)

2. God, having all life, glory, goodness, blessedness, in and of himself, is alone in and unto himself all-sufficient, not standing in need of any creature which he hath made, nor deriving any glory from them, but only manifesting his own glory in, by, unto, and upon them; he is the alone fountain of all being, of whom, through whom, and to whom are all things, and he hath most sovereign dominion over all creatures, to do by them, for them, or upon them, whatsoever himself pleaseth; in his sight all things are open and manifest, his knowledge is infinite, infallible, and independent upon the creature, so as nothing is to him contingent or uncertain; he is most holy in all his counsels, in all his works, and in all his commands; to him is due from angels and men, whatsoever worship, service, or obedience, as creatures they owe unto the Creator, and whatever he is further pleased to require of them. (John 5:26; Psalms 148:13; Psalms 119:68; Job 22:2, 3; Romans 11:34-36; Daniel 4:25, 34, 35; Hebrews 4:13; Ezekiel 11:5; Acts 15:18; Psalms 145:17; Revelation 5:12-14)

3. In this divine and infinite Being there are three subsistences, the Father, the Word or Son, and Holy Spirit, of one substance, power, and eternity, each having the whole divine essence, yet the essence undivided: the Father is of none, neither begotten nor proceeding; the Son is eternally begotten of the Father; the Holy Spirit proceeding from the Father and the Son; all infinite, without beginning, therefore but one God, who is not to be divided in nature and being, but distinguished by several peculiar relative properties and personal relations; which doctrine of the Trinity is the foundation of all our communion with God, and comfortable dependence on him. (1 John 5:7; Matthew 28:19; 2 Corinthians 13:14; Exodus 3:14; John 14:11; 1 Corinthians 8:6; John 1:14, 18; John 15:26;

Galatians 4:6)

Chapter 3: Of God's Decree

1. God hath decreed in himself, from all eternity, by the most wise and holy counsel of his own will, freely and unchangeably, all things, whatsoever comes to pass; yet so as thereby is God neither the author of sin nor hath fellowship with any therein; nor is violence offered to the will of the creature, nor yet is the liberty or contingency of second causes taken away, but rather established; in which appears his wisdom in disposing all things, and power and faithfulness in accomplishing his decree. (Isaiah 46:10; Ephesians 1:11; Hebrews 6:17; Romans 9:15, 18; James 1:13; 1 John 1:5; Acts 4:27, 28; John 19:11; Numbers 23:19; Ephesians 1:3-5)

2. Although God knoweth whatsoever may or can come to pass, upon all supposed conditions, yet hath he not decreed anything, because he foresaw it as future, or as that which would come to pass upon such conditions. (Acts 15:18; Romans 9:11, 13, 16, 18)

3. By the decree of God, for the manifestation of his glory, some men and angels are predestinated, or foreordained to eternal life through Jesus Christ, to the praise of his glorious grace; others being left to act in their sin to their just condemnation, to the praise of his glorious justice. (1 Timothy 5:21; Matthew 25:34; Ephesians 1:5, 6; Romans 9:22, 23; Jude 4)

4. These angels and men thus predestinated and foreordained, are particularly and unchangeably designed, and their number so certain and definite, that it cannot be either increased or diminished. (2 Timothy 2:19; John 13:18)

5. Those of mankind that are predestinated to life, God, before the foundation of the world was laid, according to his eternal and immutable purpose, and the secret counsel and good pleasure of his

will, hath chosen in Christ unto everlasting glory, out of his mere free grace and love, without any other thing in the creature as a condition or cause moving him thereunto. (Ephesians 1:4, 9, 11; Romans 8:30; 2 Timothy 1:9; 1 Thessalonians 5:9; Romans 9:13, 16; Ephesians 2:5, 12)

6. As God hath appointed the elect unto glory, so he hath, by the eternal and most free purpose of his will, foreordained all the means thereunto; wherefore they who are elected, being fallen in Adam, are redeemed by Christ, are effectually called unto faith in Christ, by his Spirit working in due season, are justified, adopted, sanctified, and kept by his power through faith unto salvation; neither are any other redeemed by Christ, or effectually called, justified, adopted, sanctified, and saved, but the elect only. (1 Peter 1:2; 2 Thessalonians 2:13; 1 Thessalonians 5:9, 10; Romans 8:30; 2 Thessalonians 2:13; 1 Peter 1:5; John 10:26; John 17:9; John 6:64)

7. The doctrine of the high mystery of predestination is to be handled with special prudence and care, that men attending the will of God revealed in his Word, and yielding obedience thereunto, may, from the certainty of their effectual vocation, be assured of their eternal election; so shall this doctrine afford matter of praise, reverence, and admiration of God, and of humility, diligence, and abundant consolation to all that sincerely obey the gospel. (1 Thessalonians 1:4, 5; 2 Peter 1:10; Ephesians 1:6; Romans 11:33; Romans 11:5, 6, 20; Luke 10:20)

Chapter 4: Of Creation

1. In the beginning it pleased God the Father, Son, and Holy Spirit, for the manifestation of the glory of his eternal power, wisdom, and goodness, to create or make the world, and all things therein, whether visible or invisible, in the space of six days, and all very good. (John 1:2, 3; Hebrews 1:2; Job 26:13; Romans 1:20; Colossians 1:16; Genesis 1:31)

2. After God had made all other creatures, he created man, male and female, with reasonable and immortal souls, rendering them fit unto that life to God for which they were created; being made after the image of God, in knowledge, righteousness, and true holiness; having the law of God written in their hearts, and power to fulfil it, and yet under a possibility of transgressing, being left to the liberty of their own will, which was subject to change. (Genesis 1:27; Genesis 2:7; Ecclesiastes 7:29; Genesis 1:26; Romans 2:14, 15; Genesis 3:6)

3. Besides the law written in their hearts, they received a command not to eat of the tree of knowledge of good and evil, which whilst they kept, they were happy in their communion with God, and had dominion over the creatures. (Genesis 2:17; Genesis 1:26, 28)

Chapter 5: Of Divine Providence

1. God the good Creator of all things, in his infinite power and wisdom doth uphold, direct, dispose, and govern all creatures and things, from the greatest even to the least, by his most wise and holy providence, to the end for the which they were created, according unto his infallible foreknowledge, and the free and immutable counsel of his own will; to the praise of the glory of his wisdom, power, justice, infinite goodness, and mercy. (Hebrews 1:3; Job 38:11; Isaiah 46:10, 11; Psalms 135:6; Matthew 10:29-31; Ephesians 1:11)

2. Although in relation to the foreknowledge and decree of God, the first cause, all things come to pass immutably and infallibly; so that there is not anything befalls any by chance, or without his providence; yet by the same providence he ordereth them to fall out according to the nature of second causes, either necessarily, freely, or contingently. (Acts 2:23; Proverbs 16:33; Genesis 8:22)

3. God, in his ordinary providence maketh use of means, yet is free

to work without, above, and against them at his pleasure. (Acts 27:31, 44; Isaiah 55:10, 11; Hosea 1:7; Romans 4:19-21; Daniel 3:27)

4. The almighty power, unsearchable wisdom, and infinite goodness of God, so far manifest themselves in his providence, that his determinate counsel extendeth itself even to the first fall, and all other sinful actions both of angels and men; and that not by a bare permission, which also he most wisely and powerfully boundeth, and otherwise ordereth and governeth, in a manifold dispensation to his most holy ends; yet so, as the sinfulness of their acts proceedeth only from the creatures, and not from God, who, being most holy and righteous, neither is nor can be the author or approver of sin. (Romans 11:32-34; 2 Samuel 24:1, 1 Chronicles 21:1; 2 Kings 19:28; Psalms 76;10; Genesis 1:20; Isaiah 10:6, 7, 12; Psalms 1:21; 1 John 2:16)

5. The most wise, righteous, and gracious God doth oftentimes leave for a season his own children to manifold temptations and the corruptions of their own hearts, to chastise them for their former sins, or to discover unto them the hidden strength of corruption and deceitfulness of their hearts, that they may be humbled; and to raise them to a more close and constant dependence for their support upon himself; and to make them more watchful against all future occasions of sin, and for other just and holy ends. So that whatsoever befalls any of his elect is by his appointment, for his glory, and their good. (2 Chronicles 32:25, 26, 31; 2 Corinthians 12:7-9; Romans 8:28)

6. As for those wicked and ungodly men whom God, as the righteous judge, for former sin doth blind and harden; from them he not only withholdeth his grace, whereby they might have been enlightened in their understanding, and wrought upon their hearts; but sometimes also withdraweth the gifts which they had, and exposeth them to such objects as their corruption makes occasion of sin; and withal, gives them over to their own lusts, the temptations

of the world, and the power of Satan, whereby it comes to pass that they harden themselves, under those means which God useth for the softening of others. (Romans 1:24-26, 28; Romans 11:7, 8; Deuteronomy 29:4; Matthew 13:12; Deuteronomy 2:30; 2 Kings 8:12, 13; Psalms 81:11, 12; 2 Thessalonians 2:10-12; Exodus 8:15, 32; Isaiah 6:9, 10; 1 Peter 2:7, 8)

7. As the providence of God doth in general reach to all creatures, so after a more special manner it taketh care of his church, and disposeth of all things to the good thereof. (1 Timothy 4:10; Amos 9:8, 9; Isaiah 43:3-5)

Chapter 6: Of the Fall of Man, Of Sin, And of the Punishment Thereof

1. Although God created man upright and perfect, and gave him a righteous law, which had been unto life had he kept it, and threatened death upon the breach thereof, yet he did not long abide in this honour; Satan using the subtlety of the serpent to subdue Eve, then by her seducing Adam, who, without any compulsion, did willfully transgress the law of their creation, and the command given unto them, in eating the forbidden fruit, which God was pleased, according to his wise and holy counsel to permit, having purposed to order it to his own glory. (Genesis 2:16, 17; Genesis 3:12, 13; 2 Corinthians 11:3)

2. Our first parents, by this sin, fell from their original righteousness and communion with God, and we in them whereby death came upon all: all becoming dead in sin, and wholly defiled in all the faculties and parts of soul and body. (Romans 3:23; Romans 5:12, etc.; Titus 1:15; Genesis 6:5; Jeremiah 17:9; Romans 3:10-19)

3. They being the root, and by God's appointment, standing in the room and stead of all mankind, the guilt of the sin was imputed, and corrupted nature conveyed, to all their posterity descending

from them by ordinary generation, being now conceived in sin, and by nature children of wrath, the servants of sin, the subjects of death, and all other miseries, spiritual, temporal, and eternal, unless the Lord Jesus set them free. (Romans 5:12-19; 1 Corinthians 15:21, 22, 45, 49; Psalms 51:5; Job 14:4; Ephesians 2:3; Romans 6:20 Romans 5:12; Hebrews 2:14, 15; 1 Thessalonians 1:10)

4. From this original corruption, whereby we are utterly indisposed, disabled, and made opposite to all good, and wholly inclined to all evil, do proceed all actual transgressions. (Romans 8:7; Colossians 1:21; James 1:14, 15; Matthew 15:19)

5. The corruption of nature, during this life, doth remain in those that are regenerated; and although it be through Christ pardoned and mortified, yet both itself, and the first motions thereof, are truly and properly sin. (Romans 7:18, 23; Ecclesiastes 7:20; 1 John 1:8; Romans 7:23-25; Galatians 5:17)

Chapter 7: Of God's Covenant

1. The distance between God and the creature is so great, that although reasonable creatures do owe obedience to him as their creator, yet they could never have attained the reward of life but by some voluntary condescension on God's part, which he hath been pleased to express by way of covenant. (Luke 17:10; Job 35:7, 8)

2. Moreover, man having brought himself under the curse of the law by his fall, it pleased the Lord to make a covenant of grace, wherein he freely offereth unto sinners life and salvation by Jesus Christ, requiring of them faith in him, that they may be saved; and promising to give unto all those that are ordained unto eternal life, his Holy Spirit, to make them willing and able to believe. (Genesis 2:17; Galatians 3:10; Romans 3:20, 21; Romans 8:3; Mark 16:15, 16; John 3:16; Ezekiel 36:26, 27; John 6:44, 45; Psalms 110:3)

3. This covenant is revealed in the gospel; first of all to Adam in the promise of salvation by the seed of the woman, and afterwards by farther steps, until the full discovery thereof was completed in the New Testament; and it is founded in that eternal covenant transaction that was between the Father and the Son about the redemption of the elect; and it is alone by the grace of this covenant that all the posterity of fallen Adam that ever were saved did obtain life and blessed immortality, man being now utterly incapable of acceptance with God upon those terms on which Adam stood in his state of innocency. (Genesis 3:15; Hebrews 1:1; 2 Timothy 1:9; Titus 1:2; Hebrews 11:6, 13; Romans 4:1, 2, etc.; Acts 4:12; John 8:56)

Chapter 8: Of Christ the Mediator

1. It pleased God, in His eternal purpose, to choose and ordain the Lord Jesus, his only begotten Son, according to the covenant made between them both, to be the mediator between God and man; the prophet, priest, and king; head and saviour of the church, the heir of all things, and judge of the world; unto whom he did from all eternity give a people to be his seed and to be by him in time redeemed, called, justified, sanctified, and glorified. (Isaiah 42:1; 1 Peter 1:19, 20; Acts 3:22; Hebrews 5:5, 6; Psalms 2:6; Luke 1:33; Ephesians 1:22, 23; Hebrews 1:2; Acts 17:31; Isaiah 53:10; John 17:6; Romans 8:30)

2. The Son of God, the second person in the Holy Trinity, being very and eternal God, the brightness of the Father's glory, of one substance and equal with him who made the world, who upholdeth and governeth all things he hath made, did, when the fullness of time was come, take upon him man's nature, with all the essential properties and common infirmities thereof, yet without sin; being conceived by the Holy Spirit in the womb of the Virgin Mary, the Holy Spirit coming down upon her: and the power of the Most High overshadowing her; and so was made of a woman of the tribe of Judah, of the seed of Abraham and David according to the

Scriptures; so that two whole, perfect, and distinct natures were inseparably joined together in one person, without conversion, composition, or confusion; which person is very God and very man, yet one Christ, the only mediator between God and man. (John 1:14; Galatians 4;4; Romans 8:3; Hebrews 2:14, 16, 17; Hebrews 4:15; Matthew 1:22, 23; Luke 1:27, 31, 35; Romans 9:5; 1 Timothy 2:5)

3. The Lord Jesus, in his human nature thus united to the divine, in the person of the Son, was sanctified and anointed with the Holy Spirit above measure, having in Him all the treasures of wisdom and knowledge; in whom it pleased the Father that all fullness should dwell, to the end that being holy, harmless, undefiled, and full of grace and truth, he might be throughly furnished to execute the office of mediator and surety; which office he took not upon himself, but was thereunto called by his Father; who also put all power and judgement in his hand, and gave him commandment to execute the same. (Psalms 45:7; Acts 10:38; John 3:34; Colossians 2:3; Colossians 1:19; Hebrews 7:26; John 1:14; Hebrews 7:22; Hebrews 5:5; John 5:22, 27; Matthew 28:18; Acts 2:36)

4. This office the Lord Jesus did most willingly undertake, which that he might discharge he was made under the law, and did perfectly fulfil it, and underwent the punishment due to us, which we should have borne and suffered, being made sin and a curse for us; enduring most grievous sorrows in his soul, and most painful sufferings in his body; was crucified, and died, and remained in the state of the dead, yet saw no corruption: on the third day he arose from the dead with the same body in which he suffered, with which he also ascended into heaven, and there sitteth at the right hand of his Father making intercession, and shall return to judge men and angels at the end of the world. (Psalms 40:7, 8; Hebrews 10:5-10; John 10:18; Gal 4:4; Matthew 3:15; Galatians 3:13; Isaiah 53:6; 1 Peter 3:18; 2 Corinthians 5:21; Matthew 26:37, 38; Luke 22:44; Matthew 27:46; Acts 13:37; 1 Corinthians 15:3, 4; John 20:25, 27; Mark 16:19; Acts 1:9-11; Romans 8:34; Hebrews 9:24; Acts 10:42; Romans 14:9,

10; Acts 1:11; 2 Peter 2:4)

5. The Lord Jesus, by his perfect obedience and sacrifice of himself, which he through the eternal Spirit once offered up unto God, hath fully satisfied the justice of God, procured reconciliation, and purchased an everlasting inheritance in the kingdom of heaven, for all those whom the Father hath given unto Him. (Hebrews 9:14; Hebrews 10:14; Romans 3:25, 26; John 17:2; Hebrews 9:15)

6. Although the price of redemption was not actually paid by Christ till after his incarnation, yet the virtue, efficacy, and benefit thereof were communicated to the elect in all ages, successively from the beginning of the world, in and by those promises, types, and sacrifices wherein he was revealed, and signified to be the seed which should bruise the serpent's head; and the Lamb slain from the foundation of the world, being the same yesterday, and to-day and for ever. (1 Corinthians 4:10; Hebrews 4:2; 1 Peter 1:10, 11; Revelation 13:8; Hebrews 13:8)

7. Christ, in the work of mediation, acteth according to both natures, by each nature doing that which is proper to itself; yet by reason of the unity of the person, that which is proper to one nature is sometimes in Scripture, attributed to the person denominated by the other nature. (John 3:13; Acts 20:28)

8. To all those for whom Christ hath obtained eternal redemption, he doth certainly and effectually apply and communicate the same, making intercession for them; uniting them to himself by his Spirit, revealing unto them, in and by his Word, the mystery of salvation, persuading them to believe and obey, governing their hearts by his Word and Spirit, and overcoming all their enemies by his almighty power and wisdom, in such manner and ways as are most consonant to his wonderful and unsearchable dispensation; and all of free and absolute grace, without any condition foreseen in them to procure it. (John 6:37; John 10:15, 16; John 17:9; Romans 5:10; John

17:6; Ephesians 1:9; 1 John 5:20; Romans 8:9, 14; Psalms 110:1; 1 Corinthians 15:25, 26; John 3:8; Ephesians 1:8)

9. This office of mediator between God and man is proper only to Christ, who is the prophet, priest, and king of the church of God; and may not be either in whole, or any part thereof, transferred from him to any other. (1 Timothy 2:5)

10. This number and order of offices is necessary; for in respect of our ignorance, we stand in need of his prophetical office; and in respect of our alienation from God, and imperfection of the best of our services, we need his priestly office to reconcile us and present us acceptable unto God; and in respect to our averseness and utter inability to return to God, and for our rescue and security from our spiritual adversaries, we need his kingly office to convince, subdue, draw, uphold, deliver, and preserve us to his heavenly kingdom. (John 1:18; Colossians 1:21; Galatians 5:17; John 16:8; Psalms 110:3; Luke 1:74, 75)

Chapter 9: Of Will

1. God hath endued the will of man with that natural liberty and power of acting upon choice, that it is neither forced, nor by any necessity of nature determined to do good or evil. (Matthew 17:12; James 1:14; Deuteronomy 30:19)

2. Man, in his state of innocency, had freedom and power to will and to do that which was good and well-pleasing to God, but yet was unstable, so that he might fall from it. (Ecclesiastes 7:29; Genesis 3:6)

3. Man, by his fall into a state of sin, hath wholly lost all ability of will to any spiritual good accompanying salvation; so as a natural man, being altogether averse from that good, and dead in sin, is not able by his own strength to convert himself, or to prepare himself

thereunto. (Romans 5:6; Romans 8:7; Ephesians 2:1, 5; Titus 3:3-5; John 6:44)

4. When God converts a sinner, and translates him into the state of grace, he freeth him from his natural bondage under sin, and by his grace alone enables him freely to will and to do that which is spiritually good; yet so as that by reason of his remaining corruptions, he doth not perfectly, nor only will, that which is good, but doth also will that which is evil. (Colossians 1:13; John 8:36; Philippians 2:13; Romans 7:15, 18, 19, 21, 23)

5. This will of man is made perfectly and immutably free to good alone in the state of glory only. (Ephesians 4:13)

Chapter 10: Of Effectual Calling

1. Those whom God hath predestinated unto life, he is pleased in his appointed, and accepted time, effectually to call, by his Word and Spirit, out of that state of sin and death in which they are by nature, to grace and salvation by Jesus Christ; enlightening their minds spiritually and savingly to understand the things of God; taking away their heart of stone, and giving unto them a heart of flesh; renewing their wills, and by his almighty power determining them to that which is good, and effectually drawing them to Jesus Christ; yet so as they come most freely, being made willing by his grace. (Romans 8:30; Romans 11:7; Ephesians 1:10, 11; 2 Thessalonians 2:13, 14; Ephesians 2:1-6; Acts 26:18; Ephesians 1:17, 18; Ezekiel 36:26; Deuteronomy 30:6; Ezekiel 36:27; Ephesians 1:19; Psalm 110:3; Song of Solomon 1:4)

2. This effectual call is of God's free and special grace alone, not from anything at all foreseen in man, nor from any power or agency in the creature, being wholly passive therein, being dead in sins and trespasses, until being quickened and renewed by the Holy Spirit; he is thereby enabled to answer this call, and to embrace the grace

offered and conveyed in it, and that by no less power than that which raised up Christ from the dead. (2 Timothy 1:9; Ephesians 2:8; 1 Corinthians 2:14; Ephesians 2:5; John 5:25; Ephesians 1:19, 20)

3. Elect infants dying in infancy are regenerated and saved by Christ through the Spirit; who worketh when, and where, and how he pleases; so also are all elect persons, who are incapable of being outwardly called by the ministry of the Word. (John 3:3, 5, 6; John 3:8)

4. Others not elected, although they may be called by the ministry of the Word, and may have some common operations of the Spirit, yet not being effectually drawn by the Father, they neither will nor can truly come to Christ, and therefore cannot be saved: much less can men that receive not the Christian religion be saved; be they never so diligent to frame their lives according to the light of nature and the law of that religion they do profess. (Matthew 22:14; Matthew 13:20, 21; Hebrews 6:4, 5; John 6:44, 45, 65; 1 John 2:24, 25; Acts 4:12; John 4:22; John 17:3)

Chapter 11: Of Justification

1. Those whom God effectually calleth, he also freely justifieth, not by infusing righteousness into them, but by pardoning their sins, and by accounting and accepting their persons as righteous; not for anything wrought in them, or done by them, but for Christ's sake alone; not by imputing faith itself, the act of believing, or any other evangelical obedience to them, as their righteousness; but by imputing Christ's active obedience unto the whole law, and passive obedience in his death for their whole and sole righteousness by faith, which faith they have not of themselves; it is the gift of God. (Romans 3:24; Romans 8:30; Romans 4:5-8; Ephesians 1:7; 1 Corinthians 1:30, 31; Romans 5:17-19; Philippians 3:8, 9; Ephesians 2:8-10; John 1:12; Romans 5:17)

2. Faith thus receiving and resting on Christ and his righteousness, is the alone instrument of justification; yet it is not alone in the person justified, but is ever accompanied with all other saving graces, and is no dead faith, but worketh by love. (Romans 3:28; Galatians 5:6; James 2:17, 22, 26)

3. Christ, by his obedience and death, did fully discharge the debt of all those that are justified; and did, by the sacrifice of himself in the blood of his cross, undergoing in their stead the penalty due unto them, make a proper, real, and full satisfaction to God's justice in their behalf; yet, inasmuch as he was given by the Father for them, and his obedience and satisfaction accepted in their stead, and both freely, not for anything in them, their justification is only of free grace, that both the exact justice and rich grace of God might be glorified in the justification of sinners. (Hebrews 10:14; 1 Peter 1:18, 19; Isaiah 53:5, 6; Romans 8:32; 2 Corinthians 5:21; Romans 3:26; Ephesians 1:6, 7; Ephesians 2:7)

4. God did from all eternity decree to justify all the elect, and Christ did in the fullness of time die for their sins, and rise again for their justification; nevertheless, they are not justified personally, until the Holy Spirit doth in time due actually apply Christ unto them. (Galatians 3:8; 1 Peter 1:2; 1 Timothy 2:6; Romans 4:25; Colossians 1:21,22; Titus 3:4-7)

5. God doth continue to forgive the sins of those that are justified, and although they can never fall from the state of justification, yet they may, by their sins, fall under God's fatherly displeasure; and in that condition they have not usually the light of his countenance restored unto them, until they humble themselves, confess their sins, beg pardon, and renew their faith and repentance. (Matthew 6:12; 1 John 1:7, 9; John 10:28; Psalms 89:31-33; Psalms 32:5; Psalms 51; Matthew 26:75)

6. The justification of believers under the Old Testament was, in all

these respects, one and the same with the justification of believers under the New Testament. (Galatians 3:9; Romans 4:22-24)

Chapter 12: Of Adoption

All those that are justified, God vouchsafed, in and for the sake of his only Son Jesus Christ, to make partakers of the grace of adoption, by which they are taken into the number, and enjoy the liberties and privileges of the children of God, have his name put upon them, receive the spirit of adoption, have access to the throne of grace with boldness, are enabled to cry Abba, Father, are pitied, protected, provided for, and chastened by him as by a Father, yet never cast off, but sealed to the day of redemption, and inherit the promises as heirs of everlasting salvation. (Ephesians 1:5; Galatians 4:4, 5; John 1:12; Romans 8:17; 2 Corinthians 6:18; Revelation 3:12; Romans 8:15; Galatians 4:6; Ephesians 2:18; Psalms 103:13; Proverbs 14:26; 1 Peter 5:7; Hebrews 12:6; Isaiah 54:8, 9; Lamentations 3:31; Ephesians 4:30; Hebrews 1:14; Hebrews 6:12)

Chapter 13: Of Sanctification

1. They who are united to Christ, effectually called, and regenerated, having a new heart and a new spirit created in them through the virtue of Christ's death and resurrection, are also farther sanctified, really and personally, through the same virtue, by His Word and Spirit dwelling in them; the dominion of the whole body of sin is destroyed, and the several lusts thereof are more and more weakened and mortified, and they more and more quickened and strengthened in all saving graces, to the practice of all true holiness, without which no man shall see the Lord. (Acts 20:32; Romans 6:5, 6; John 17:17; Ephesians 3:16-19; 1 Thessalonians 5:21-23; Romans 6:14; Galatians 5:24; Colossians 1:11; 2 Corinthians 7:1; Hebrews 12:14)

2. This sanctification is throughout the whole man, yet imperfect in

this life; there abideth still some remnants of corruption in every part, whence ariseth a continual and irreconcilable war; the flesh lusting against the Spirit, and the Spirit against the flesh. (1 Thessalonians 5:23; Romans 7:18, 23; Galatians 5:17; 1 Peter 2:11)

3. In which war, although the remaining corruption for a time may much prevail, yet through the continual supply of strength from the sanctifying Spirit of Christ, the regenerate part doth overcome; and so the saints grow in grace, perfecting holiness in the fear of God, pressing after an heavenly life, in evangelical obedience to all the commands which Christ as Head and King, in His Word hath prescribed them. (Romans 7:23; Romans 6:14; Ephesians 4:15, 16; 2 Corinthians 3:18; 2 Corinthians 7:1)

Chapter 14: Of Saving Faith

1. The grace of faith, whereby the elect are enabled to believe to the saving of their souls, is the work of the Spirit of Christ in their hearts, and is ordinarily wrought by the ministry of the Word; by which also, and by the administration of baptism and the Lord's supper, prayer, and other means appointed of God, it is increased and strengthened. (2 Corinthians 4:13; Ephesians 2:8; Romans 10:14, 17; Luke 17:5; 1 Peter 2:2; Acts 20:32)

2. By this faith a Christian believeth to be true whatsoever is revealed in the Word for the authority of God himself, and also apprehendeth an excellency therein above all other writings and all things in the world, as it bears forth the glory of God in his attributes, the excellency of Christ in his nature and offices, and the power and fullness of the Holy Spirit in his workings and operations: and so is enabled to cast his soul upon the truth thus believed; and also acteth differently upon that which each particular passage thereof containeth; yielding obedience to the commands, trembling at the threatenings, and embracing the promises of God for this life and that which is to come; but the

principal acts of saving faith have immediate relation to Christ, accepting, receiving, and resting upon him alone for justification, sanctification, and eternal life, by virtue of the covenant of grace. (Acts 24:14; Psalms 27:7-10; Psalms 119:72; 2 Timothy 1:12; John 14:14; Isaiah 66:2; Hebrews 11:13; John 1:12; Acts 16:31; Galatians 2:20; Acts 15:11)

3. This faith, although it be different in degrees, and may be weak or strong, yet it is in the least degree of it different in the kind or nature of it, as is all other saving grace, from the faith and common grace of temporary believers; and therefore, though it may be many times assailed and weakened, yet it gets the victory, growing up in many to the attainment of a full assurance through Christ, who is both the author and finisher of our faith. (Hebrews 5:13, 14; Matthew 6:30; Romans 4:19, 20; 2 Peter 1:1; Ephesians 6:16; 1 John 5:4, 5; Hebrews 6:11, 12; Colossians 2:2; Hebrews 12:2)

Chapter 15: Of Repentance Unto Life and Salvation

1. Such of the elect as are converted at riper years, having sometime lived in the state of nature, and therein served divers lusts and pleasures, God in their effectual calling giveth them repentance unto life. (Titus 3:2-5)

2. Whereas there is none that doth good and sinneth not, and the best of men may, through the power and deceitfulness of their corruption dwelling in them, with the prevalency of temptation, fall into great sins and provocations; God hath, in the covenant of grace, mercifully provided that believers so sinning and falling be renewed through repentance unto salvation. (Ecclesiastes 7:20; Luke 22:31, 32)

3. This saving repentance is an evangelical grace, whereby a person, being by the Holy Spirit made sensible of the manifold evils of his sin, doth, by faith in Christ, humble himself for it with godly

sorrow, detestation of it, and self-abhorrency, praying for pardon and strength of grace, with a purpose and endeavour, by supplies of the Spirit, to walk before God unto all well-pleasing in all things. (Zechariah 12:10; Acts 11:18; Ezekiel 36:31; 2 Corinthians 7:11; Psalms 119:6; Psalms 119:128)

4. As repentance is to be continued through the whole course of our lives, upon the account of the body of death, and the motions thereof, so it is every man's duty to repent of his particular known sins particularly. (Luke 19:8; 1 Timothy 1:13, 15)

5. Such is the provision which God hath made through Christ in the covenant of grace for the preservation of believers unto salvation; that although there is no sin so small but it deserves damnation; yet there is no sin so great that it shall bring damnation on them that repent; which makes the constant preaching of repentance necessary. (Romans 6:23; Isaiah 1:16-18 Isaiah 55:7)

Chapter 16: Of Good Works

1. Good works are only such as God hath commanded in his Holy Word, and not such as without the warrant thereof are devised by men out of blind zeal, or upon any pretence of good intentions. (Micah 6:8; Hebrews 13:21; Matthew 15:9; Isaiah 29:13)

2. These good works, done in obedience to God's commandments, are the fruits and evidences of a true and lively faith; and by them believers manifest their thankfulness, strengthen their assurance, edify their brethren, adorn the profession of the gospel, stop the mouths of the adversaries, and glorify God, whose workmanship they are, created in Christ Jesus thereunto, that having their fruit unto holiness they may have the end eternal life. (James 2:18, 22; Psalms 116:12, 13; 1 John 2:3, 5; 2 Peter 1:5-11; Matthew 5:16; 1 Timothy 6:1; 1 Peter 2:15; Philippians 1:11; Ephesians 2:10; Romans 6:22)

3. Their ability to do good works is not at all of themselves, but wholly from the Spirit of Christ; and that they may be enabled thereunto, besides the graces they have already received, there is necessary an actual influence of the same Holy Spirit, to work in them to will and to do of his good pleasure; yet they are not hereupon to grow negligent, as if they were not bound to perform any duty, unless upon a special motion of the Spirit, but they ought to be diligent in stirring up the grace of God that is in them. (John 15:4, 5; 2 Corinthians 3:5; Philippians 2:13; Philippians 2:12; Hebrews 6:11, 12; Isaiah 64:7)

4. They who in their obedience attain to the greatest height which is possible in this life, are so far from being able to supererogate, and to do more than God requires, as that they fall short of much which in duty they are bound to do. (Job 9:2, 3; Galatians 5:17; Luke 17:10)

5. We cannot by our best works merit pardon of sin or eternal life at the hand of God, by reason of the great disproportion that is between them and the glory to come, and the infinite distance that is between us and God, whom by them we can neither profit nor satisfy for the debt of our former sins; but when we have done all we can, we have done but our duty, and are unprofitable servants; and because as they are good they proceed from his Spirit, and as they are wrought by us they are defiled and mixed with so much weakness and imperfection, that they cannot endure the severity of God's punishment. (Romans 3:20; Ephesians 2:8, 9; Romans 4:6; Galatians 5:22, 23; Isaiah 64:6; Psalms 143:2)

6. Yet notwithstanding the persons of believers being accepted through Christ, their good works also are accepted in him; not as though they were in this life wholly unblameable and unreprovable in God's sight, but that he, looking upon them in his Son, is pleased to accept and reward that which is sincere, although accompanied with many weaknesses and imperfections. (Ephesians 1:6; 1 Peter 2:5; Matthew 25:21, 23; Hebrews 6:10)

7. Works done by unregenerate men, although for the matter of them they may be things which God commands, and of good use both to themselves and others; yet because they proceed not from a heart purified by faith, nor are done in a right manner according to the word, nor to a right end, the glory of God, they are therefore sinful, and cannot please God, nor make a man meet to receive grace from God, and yet their neglect of them is more sinful and displeasing to God. (2 Kings 10:30; 1 Kings 21:27, 29; Genesis 4:5; Hebrews 11:4, 6; 1 Corinthians 13:1; Matthew 6:2, 5; Amos 5:21, 22; Romans 9:16; Titus 3:5; Job 21:14, 15; Matthew 25:41-43)

Chapter 17: Of The Perseverance of the Saint

1. Those whom God hath accepted in the beloved, effectually called and sanctified by his Spirit, and given the precious faith of his elect unto, can neither totally nor finally fall from the state of grace, but shall certainly persevere therein to the end, and be eternally saved, seeing the gifts and callings of God are without repentance, whence he still begets and nourisheth in them faith, repentance, love, joy, hope, and all the graces of the Spirit unto immortality; and though many storms and floods arise and beat against them, yet they shall never be able to take them off that foundation and rock which by faith they are fastened upon; notwithstanding, through unbelief and the temptations of Satan, the sensible sight of the light and love of God may for a time be clouded and obscured from them, yet he is still the same, and they shall be sure to be kept by the power of God unto salvation, where they shall enjoy their purchased possession, they being engraven upon the palm of his hands, and their names having been written in the book of life from all eternity. (John 10:28, 29; Philippians 1:6; 2 Timothy 2:19; 1 John 2:19; Psalms 89:31, 32; 1 Corinthians 11:32; Malachi 3:6)

2. This perseverance of the saints depends not upon their own free will, but upon the immutability of the decree of election, flowing from the free and unchangeable love of God the Father, upon the

efficacy of the merit and intercession of Jesus Christ and union with him, the oath of God, the abiding of his Spirit, and the seed of God within them, and the nature of the covenant of grace; from all which ariseth also the certainty and infallibility thereof. (Romans 8:30 Romans 9:11, 16; Romans 5:9, 10; John 14:19; Hebrews 6:17, 18; 1 John 3:9; Jeremiah 32:40)

3. And though they may, through the temptation of Satan and of the world, the prevalency of corruption remaining in them, and the neglect of means of their preservation, fall into grievous sins, and for a time continue therein, whereby they incur God's displeasure and grieve his Holy Spirit, come to have their graces and comforts impaired, have their hearts hardened, and their consciences wounded, hurt and scandalize others, and bring temporal judgments upon themselves, yet shall they renew their repentance and be preserved through faith in Christ Jesus to the end. (Matthew 26:70, 72, 74; Isaiah 64:5, 9; Ephesians 4:30; Psalms 51:10, 12; Psalms 32:3, 4; 2 Samuel 12:14; Luke 22:32, 61, 62)

Chapter 18: Of the Assurance of Grace and Salvation

1. Although temporary believers, and other unregenerate men, may vainly deceive themselves with false hopes and carnal presumptions of being in the favour of God and state of salvation, which hope of theirs shall perish; yet such as truly believe in the Lord Jesus, and love him in sincerity, endeavouring to walk in all good conscience before him, may in this life be certainly assured that they are in the state of grace, and may rejoice in the hope of the glory of God, which hope shall never make them ashamed. (Job 8:13, 14; Matthew 7:22, 23; 1 John 2:3; 1 John 3:14, 18, 19, 21, 24; 1 John 5:13; Romans 5:2, 5)

2. This certainty is not a bare conjectural and probable persuasion grounded upon a fallible hope, but an infallible assurance of faith founded on the blood and righteousness of Christ revealed in the

Gospel; and also upon the inward evidence of those graces of the Spirit unto which promises are made, and on the testimony of the Spirit of adoption, witnessing with our spirits that we are the children of God; and, as a fruit thereof, keeping the heart both humble and holy. (Hebrews 6:11, 19; Hebrews 6:17, 18; 2 Peter 1:4, 5, 10, 11; Romans 8:15, 16; 1 John 3:1-3)

3. This infallible assurance doth not so belong to the essence of faith, but that a true believer may wait long, and conflict with many difficulties before he be partaker of it; yet being enabled by the Spirit to know the things which are freely given him of God, he may, without extraordinary revelation, in the right use of means, attain thereunto: and therefore it is the duty of every one to give all diligence to make his calling and election sure, that thereby his heart may be enlarged in peace and joy in the Holy Spirit, in love and thankfulness to God, and in strength and cheerfulness in the duties of obedience, the proper fruits of this assurance; -so far is it from inclining men to looseness. (Isaiah 50:10; Psalms 88; Psalms 77:1-12; 1 John 4:13; Hebrews 6:11, 12; Romans 5:1, 2, 5; Romans 14:17; Psalms 119:32; Romans 6:1, 2; Titus 2:11, 12, 14)

4. True believers may have the assurance of their salvation divers ways shaken, diminished, and intermitted; as by negligence in preserving of it, by falling into some special sin which woundeth the conscience and grieveth the Spirit; by some sudden or vehement temptation, by God's withdrawing the light of his countenance, and suffering even such as fear him to walk in darkness and to have no light, yet are they never destitute of the seed of God and life of faith, that love of Christ and the brethren, that sincerity of heart and conscience of duty out of which, by the operation of the Spirit, this assurance may in due time be revived, and by the which, in the meantime, they are preserved from utter despair. (Song of Solomon 5:2, 3, 6; Psalms 51:8, 12, 14; Psalms 116:11; Psalms 77:7, 8; Psalms 31:22; Psalms 30:7; 1 John 3:9; Luke 22:32; Psalms 42:5, 11; Lamentations 3:26-31)

Chapter 19: Of the Law of God

1. God gave to Adam a law of universal obedience written in his heart, and a particular precept of not eating the fruit of the tree of knowledge of good and evil; by which he bound him and all his posterity to personal, entire, exact, and perpetual obedience; promised life upon the fulfilling, and threatened death upon the breach of it, and endued him with power and ability to keep it. (Genesis 1:27; Ecclesiastes 7:29; Romans 10:5; Galatians 3:10, 12)

2. The same law that was first written in the heart of man continued to be a perfect rule of righteousness after the fall, and was delivered by God upon Mount Sinai, in ten commandments, and written in two tables, the four first containing our duty towards God, and the other six, our duty to man. (Romans 2:14, 15; Deuteronomy 10:4)

3. Besides this law, commonly called moral, God was pleased to give to the people of Israel ceremonial laws, containing several typical ordinances, partly of worship, prefiguring Christ, his graces, actions, sufferings, and benefits; and partly holding forth divers instructions of moral duties, all which ceremonial laws being appointed only to the time of reformation, are, by Jesus Christ the true Messiah and only law-giver, who was furnished with power from the Father for that end abrogated and taken away. (Hebrews 10:1; Colossians 2:17; 1 Corinthians 5:7; Colossians 2:14, 16, 17; Ephesians 2:14, 16)

4. To them also he gave sundry judicial laws, which expired together with the state of that people, not obliging any now by virtue of that institution; their general equity only being of moral use. (1 Corinthians 9:8-10)

5. The moral law doth for ever bind all, as well justified persons as others, to the obedience thereof, and that not only in regard of the matter contained in it, but also in respect of the authority of God the

Creator, who gave it; neither doth Christ in the Gospel any way dissolve, but much strengthen this obligation. (Romans 13:8-10; James 2:8, 10-12; James 2:10, 11; Matthew 5:17-19; Romans 3:31)

6. Although true believers be not under the law as a covenant of works, to be thereby justified or condemned, yet it is of great use to them as well as to others, in that as a rule of life, informing them of the will of God and their duty, it directs and binds them to walk accordingly; discovering also the sinful pollutions of their natures, hearts, and lives, so as examining themselves thereby, they may come to further conviction of, humiliation for, and hatred against, sin; together with a clearer sight of the need they have of Christ and the perfection of his obedience; it is likewise of use to the regenerate to restrain their corruptions, in that it forbids sin; and the threatenings of it serve to shew what even their sins deserve, and what afflictions in this life they may expect for them, although freed from the curse and unallayed rigour thereof. The promises of it likewise shew them God's approbation of obedience, and what blessings they may expect upon the performance thereof, though not as due to them by the law as a covenant of works; so as man's doing good and refraining from evil, because the law encourageth to the one and deterreth from the other, is no evidence of his being under the law and not under grace. (Romans 6:14; Galatians 2:16; Romans 8:1; Romans 10:4; Romans 3:20; Romans 7:7, etc.; Romans 6:12-14; 1 Peter 3:8-13)

7. Neither are the aforementioned uses of the law contrary to the grace of the Gospel, but do sweetly comply with it, the Spirit of Christ subduing and enabling the will of man to do that freely and cheerfully which the will of God, revealed in the law, requireth to be done. (Galatians 3:21; Ezekiel 36:27)

Chapter 20: Of the Gospel, and of the Extent of the Grace Thereof

1. The covenant of works being broken by sin, and made

unprofitable unto life, God was pleased to give forth the promise of Christ, the seed of the woman, as the means of calling the elect, and begetting in them faith and repentance; in this promise the gospel, as to the substance of it, was revealed, and [is] therein effectual for the conversion and salvation of sinners. (Genesis 3:15; Revelation 13:8)

2. This promise of Christ, and salvation by him, is revealed only by the Word of God; neither do the works of creation or providence, with the light of nature, make discovery of Christ, or of grace by him, so much as in a general or obscure way; much less that men destitute of the revelation of Him by the promise or gospel, should be enabled thereby to attain saving faith or repentance. (Romans 1:17; Romans 10:14, 15, 17; Proverbs 29:18; Isaiah 25:7; Isaiah 60:2, 3)

3. The revelation of the gospel unto sinners, made in divers times and by sundry parts, with the addition of promises and precepts for the obedience required therein, as to the nations and persons to whom it is granted, is merely of the sovereign will and good pleasure of God; not being annexed by virtue of any promise to the due improvement of men's natural abilities, by virtue of common light received without it, which none ever did make, or can do so; and therefore in all ages, the preaching of the gospel has been granted unto persons and nations, as to the extent or straitening of it, in great variety, according to the counsel of the will of God. (Psalms 147:20; Acts 16:7; Romans 1:18-32)

4. Although the gospel be the only outward means of revealing Christ and saving grace, and is, as such, abundantly sufficient thereunto; yet that men who are dead in trespasses may be born again, quickened or regenerated, there is moreover necessary an effectual insuperable work of the Holy Spirit upon the whole soul, for the producing in them a new spiritual life; without which no other means will effect their conversion unto God. (Psalms 110:3; 1 Corinthians 2:14; Ephesians 1:19, 20; John 6:44; 2 Corinthians 4:4, 6)

Chapter 21: Of Christian Liberty and Liberty of Conscience

1. The liberty which Christ hath purchased for believers under the gospel, consists in their freedom from the guilt of sin, the condemning wrath of God, the rigour and curse of the law, and in their being delivered from this present evil world, bondage to Satan, and dominion of sin, from the evil of afflictions, the fear and sting of death, the victory of the grave, and ever- lasting damnation: as also in their free access to God, and their yielding obedience unto Him, not out of slavish fear, but a child-like love and willing mind. All which were common also to believers under the law for the substance of them; but under the New Testament the liberty of Christians is further enlarged, in their freedom from the yoke of a ceremonial law, to which the Jewish church was subjected, and in greater boldness of access to the throne of grace, and in fuller communications of the free Spirit of God, than believers under the law did ordinarily partake of. (Galatians 3:13; Galatians 1:4; Acts 26:18; Romans 8:3; Romans 8:28; 1 Corinthians 15:54-57; 2 Thessalonians 1:10; Romans 8:15; Luke 1:73-75; 1 John 4:18; Galatians 3:9, 14; John 7:38, 39; Hebrews 10:19-21)

2. God alone is Lord of the conscience, and hath left it free from the doctrines and commandments of men which are in any thing contrary to his word, or not contained in it. So that to believe such doctrines, or obey such commands out of conscience, is to betray true liberty of conscience; and the requiring of an implicit faith, an absolute and blind obedience, is to destroy liberty of conscience and reason also. (James 4:12; Romans 14:4; Acts 4:19, 29; 1 Corinthians 7:23; Matthew 15:9; Colossians 2:20, 22, 23; 1 Corinthians 3:5; 2 Corinthians 1:24)

3. They who upon pretence of Christian liberty do practice any sin, or cherish any sinful lust, as they do thereby pervert the main design of the grace of the gospel to their own destruction, so they wholly destroy the end of Christian liberty, which is, that being

delivered out of the hands of all our enemies, we might serve the Lord without fear, in holiness and righeousness before Him, all the days of our lives. (Romans 6:1, 2; Galatians 5:13; 2 Peter 2:18, 21)

Chapter 22: Of Religious Worship and the Sabbath Day

1. The light of nature shews that there is a God, who hath lordship and sovereignty over all; is just, good and doth good unto all; and is therefore to be feared, loved, praised, called upon, trusted in, and served, with all the heart and all the soul, and with all the might. But the acceptable way of worshipping the true God, is instituted by himself, and so limited by his own revealed will, that he may not be worshipped according to the imagination and devices of men, nor the suggestions of Satan, under any visible representations, or any other way not prescribed in the Holy Scriptures. (Jeremiah 10:7; Mark 12:33; Deuteronomy 12:32; Exodus 20:4-6)

2. Religious worship is to be given to God the Father, Son, and Holy Spirit, and to him alone; not to angels, saints, or any other creatures; and since the fall, not without a mediator, nor in the mediation of any other but Christ alone. (Matthew 4:9, 10; John 6:23; Matthew 28:19; Romans 1:25; Colossians 2:18; Revelation 19:10; John 14:6; 1 Timothy 2:5)

3. Prayer, with thanksgiving, being one part of natural worship, is by God required of all men. But that it may be accepted, it is to be made in the name of the Son, by the help of the Spirit, according to his will; with understanding, reverence, humility, fervency, faith, love, and perseverance; and when with others, in a known tongue. (Psalms 95:1-7; Psalms 65:2; John 14:13, 14; Romans 8:26; 1 John 5:14; 1 Corinthians 14:16, 17)

4. Prayer is to be made for things lawful, and for all sorts of men living, or that shall live hereafter; but not for the dead, nor for those of whom it may be known that they have sinned the sin unto death.

(1 Timothy 2:1, 2; 2 Samuel 7:29; 2 Samuel 12:21-23; 1 John 5:16)

5. The reading of the Scriptures, preaching, and hearing the Word of God, teaching and admonishing one another in psalms, hymns, and spiritual songs, singing with grace in our hearts to the Lord; as also the administration of baptism, and the Lord's supper, are all parts of religious worship of God, to be performed in obedience to him, with understanding, faith, reverence, and godly fear; moreover, solemn humiliation, with fastings, and thanksgivings, upon special occasions, ought to be used in an holy and religious manner. (1 Timothy 4:13; 2 Timothy 4:2; Luke 8:18; Colossians 3:16; Ephesians 5:19; Matthew 28:19, 20; 1 Corinthians 11:26; Esther 4:16; Joel 2:12; Exodus 15:1-19, Psalms 107)

6. Neither prayer nor any other part of religious worship, is now under the gospel, tied unto, or made more acceptable by any place in which it is performed, or towards which it is directed; but God is to be worshipped everywhere in spirit and in truth; as in private families daily, and in secret each one by himself; so more solemnly in the public assemblies, which are not carelessly nor wilfully to be neglected or forsaken, when God by his word or providence calleth thereunto. (John 4:21; Malachi 1:11; 1 Timothy 2:8; Acts 10:2; Matthew 6:11; Psalms 55:17; Matthew 6:6; Hebrews 10:25; Acts 2:42)

7. As it is the law of nature, that in general a proportion of time, by God's appointment, be set apart for the worship of God, so by his Word, in a positive moral, and perpetual commandment, binding all men, in all ages, he hath particularly appointed one day in seven for a sabbath to be kept holy unto him, which from the beginning of the world to the resurrection of Christ was the last day of the week, and from the resurrection of Christ was changed into the first day of the week, which is called the Lord's day: and is to be continued to the end of the world as the Christian Sabbath, the observation of the last day of the week being abolished. (Exodus 20:8; 1 Corinthians 16:1, 2; Acts 20:7; Revelation 1:10)

8. The sabbath is then kept holy unto the Lord, when men, after a due preparing of their hearts, and ordering their common affairs aforehand, do not only observe an holy rest all day, from their own works, words and thoughts, about their worldly employment and recreations, but are also taken up the whole time in the public and private exercises of his worship, and in the duties of necessity and mercy. (Isaiah 58:13; Nehemiah 13:15-22; Matthew 12:1-13)

Chapter 23: Of Lawful Oaths and Vow

1. A lawful oath is a part of religious worship, wherein the person swearing in truth, righteousness, and judgement, solemnly calleth God to witness what he sweareth, and to judge him according to the truth or falseness thereof. (Exodus 20:7; Deuteronomy 10:20; Jeremiah 4:2; 2 Chronicles 6:22, 23)

2. The name of God only is that by which men ought to swear; and therein it is to be used, with all holy fear and reverence; therefore to swear vainly or rashly by that glorious and dreadful name, or to swear at all by any other thing, is sinful, and to be abhorred; yet as in matter of weight and moment, for confirmation of truth, and ending all strife, an oath is warranted by the word of God; so a lawful oath being imposed by lawful authority in such matters, ought to be taken. (Matthew 5:34, 37; James 5:12; Hebrews 6:16; 2 Corinthians 1:23; Nehemiah 13:25)

3. Whosoever taketh an oath warranted by the Word of God, ought duly to consider the weightiness of so solemn an act, and therein to avouch nothing but what he knoweth to be truth; for that by rash, false, and vain oaths, the Lord is provoked, and for them this land mourns. (Leviticus 19:12; Jeremiah 23:10)

4. An oath is to be taken in the plain and common sense of the words, without equivocation or mental reservation. (Psalms 24:4)

5. A vow, which is not to be made to any creature, but to God alone, is to be made and performed with all religious care and faithfulness; but popish monastical vows of perpetual single life, professed poverty, and regular obedience, are so far from being degrees of higher perfection, that they are superstitious and sinful snares, in which no Christian may entangle himself. (Psalms 76:11; Genesis 28:20-22; 1 Corinthians 7:2, 9; Ephesians 4:28; Matthew 19:11)

Chapter 24: Of the Civil Magistrate

1. God, the supreme Lord and King of all the world, hath ordained civil magistrates to be under him, over the people, for his own glory and the public good; and to this end hath armed them with the power of the sword, for defence and encouragement of them that do good, and for the punishment of evil doers. (Romans 13:1-4)

2. It is lawful for Christians to accept and execute the office of a magistrate when called there unto; in the management whereof, as they ought especially to maintain justice and peace, according to the wholesome laws of each kingdom and commonwealth, so for that end they may lawfully now, under the New Testament wage war upon just and necessary occasions. (2 Samuel 23:3; Psalms 82:3, 4; Luke 3:14)

3. Civil magistrates being set up by God for the ends aforesaid; subjection, in all lawful things commanded by them, ought to be yielded by us in the Lord, not only for wrath, but for conscience sake; and we ought to make supplications and prayers for kings and all that are in authority, that under them we may live a quiet and peaceable life, in all godliness and honesty. (Romans 13:5-7; 1 Peter 2:17; 1 Timothy 2:1, 2)

Chapter 25: Of Marriage

1. Marriage is to be between one man and one woman; neither is it

lawful for any man to have more than one wife, nor for any woman to have more than one husband at the same time. (Genesis 2:24; Malachi 2:15; Matthew 19:5, 6)

2. Marriage was ordained for the mutual help of husband and wife, for the increase of mankind with a legitimate issue, and the preventing of uncleanness. (Genesis 2:18; Genesis 1:28; 1 Corinthians 7:2, 9)

3. It is lawful for all sorts of people to marry, who are able with judgment to give their consent; yet it is the duty of Christians to marry in the Lord; and therefore such as profess the true religion, should not marry with infidels, or idolaters; neither should such as are godly, be unequally yoked, by marrying with such as are wicked in their life, or maintain damnable heresy. (Hebrews 13:4; 1 Timothy 4:3; 1 Corinthians 7:39; Nehemiah 13:25-27)

4. Marriage ought not to be within the degrees of consanguinity or affinity, forbidden in the Word; nor can such incestuous marriages ever be made lawful, by any law of man or consent of parties, so as those persons may live together as man and wife. (Leviticus 18; Mark 6:18; 1 Corinthians 5:1)

Chapter 26: Of the Church

1. The catholic or universal church, which (with respect to the internal work of the Spirit and truth of grace) may be called invisible, consists of the whole number of the elect, that have been, are, or shall be gathered into one, under Christ, the head thereof; and is the spouse, the body, the fulness of him that filleth all in all. (Hebrews 12:23; Colossians 1:18; Ephesians 1:10, 22, 23; Ephesians 5:23, 27, 32)

2. All persons throughout the world, professing the faith of the gospel, and obedience unto God by Christ according unto it, not

destroying their own profession by any errors everting the foundation, or unholiness of conversation, are and may be called visible saints; and of such ought all particular congregations to be constituted. (1 Corinthians 1:2; Acts 11:26; Romans 1:7; Ephesians 1:20-22)

3. The purest churches under heaven are subject to mixture and error; and some have so degenerated as to become no churches of Christ, but synagogues of Satan; nevertheless Christ always hath had, and ever shall have a kingdom in this world, to the end thereof, of such as believe in him, and make profession of his name. (1 Corinthians 5; Revelation 2; Revelation 3; Revelation 18:2; 2 Thessalonians 2:11, 12; Matthew 16:18; Psalms 72:17; Psalm 102:28; Revelation 12:17)

4. The Lord Jesus Christ is the Head of the church, in whom, by the appointment of the Father, all power for the calling, institution, order or government of the church, is invested in a supreme and sovereign manner; neither can the Pope of Rome in any sense be head thereof, but is that antichrist, that man of sin, and son of perdition, that exalteth himself in the church against Christ, and all that is called God; whom the Lord shall destroy with the brightness of his coming. (Colossians 1:18; Matthew 28:18-20; Ephesians 4:11, 12; 2 Thessalonians 2:2-9)

5. In the execution of this power wherewith he is so intrusted, the Lord Jesus calleth out of the world unto himself, through the ministry of his word, by his Spirit, those that are given unto him by his Father, that they may walk before him in all the ways of obedience, which he prescribeth to them in his word. Those thus called, he commandeth to walk together in particular societies, or churches, for their mutual edification, and the due performance of that public worship, which he requireth of them in the world. (John 10:16; John 12:32; Matthew 28:20; Matthew 18:15-20)

6. The members of these churches are saints by calling, visibly manifesting and evidencing (in and by their profession and walking) their obedience unto that call of Christ; and do willingly consent to walk together, according to the appointment of Christ; giving up themselves to the Lord, and one to another, by the will of God, in professed subjection to the ordinances of the Gospel. (Romans. 1:7; 1 Corinthians 1:2; Acts 2:41, 42; Acts 5:13, 14; 2 Corinthians 9:13)

7. To each of these churches thus gathered, according to his mind declared in his word, he hath given all that power and authority, which is in any way needful for their carrying on that order in worship and discipline, which he hath instituted for them to observe; with commands and rules for the due and right exerting, and executing of that power. (Matthew 18:17, 18; 1 Corinthians 5:4, 5; 1 Corinthians 5:13; 2 Corinthians 2:6-8)

8. A particular church, gathered and completely organized according to the mind of Christ, consists of officers and members; and the officers appointed by Christ to be chosen and set apart by the church (so called and gathered), for the peculiar administration of ordinances, and execution of power or duty, which he intrusts them with, or calls them to, to be continued to the end of the world, are bishops or elders, and deacons. (Acts 20:17, 28; Philippians 1:1)

9. The way appointed by Christ for the calling of any person, fitted and gifted by the Holy Spirit, unto the office of bishop or elder in a church, is, that he be chosen thereunto by the common suffrage of the church itself; and solemnly set apart by fasting and prayer, with imposition of hands of the eldership of the church, if there be any before constituted therein; and of a deacon that he be chosen by the like suffrage, and set apart by prayer, and the like imposition of hands. (Acts 14:23; 1 Timothy 4:14; Acts 6:3, 5, 6)

10. The work of pastors being constantly to attend the service of

Christ, in his churches, in the ministry of the word and prayer, with watching for their souls, as they that must give an account to Him; it is incumbent on the churches to whom they minister, not only to give them all due respect, but also to communicate to them of all their good things according to their ability, so as they may have a comfortable supply, without being themselves entangled in secular affairs; and may also be capable of exercising hospitality towards others; and this is required by the law of nature, and by the express order of our Lord Jesus, who hath ordained that they that preach the Gospel should live of the Gospel. (Acts 6:4; Hebrews 13:17; 1 Timothy 5:17, 18; Galatians 6:6, 7; 2 Timothy 2:4; 1 Timothy 3:2; 1 Corinthians 9:6-14)

11. Although it be incumbent on the bishops or pastors of the churches, to be instant in preaching the word, by way of office, yet the work of preaching the word is not so peculiarly confined to them but that others also gifted and fitted by the Holy Spirit for it, and approved and called by the church, may and ought to perform it. (Acts 11:19-21; 1 Peter 4:10, 11)

12. As all believers are bound to join themselves to particular churches, when and where they have opportunity so to do; so all that are admitted unto the privileges of a church, are also under the censures and government thereof, according to the rule of Christ. (1 Thessalonians 5:14; 2 Thessalonians 3:6, 14, 15)

13. No church members, upon any offence taken by them, having performed their duty required of them towards the person they are offended at, ought to disturb any church-order, or absent themselves from the assemblies of the church, or administration of any ordinances, upon the account of such offence at any of their fellow members, but to wait upon Christ, in the further proceeding of the church. (Matthew 18:15-17; Ephesians 4:2, 3)

14. As each church, and all the members of it, are bound to pray

continually for the good and prosperity of all the churches of Christ, in all places, and upon all occasions to further it (every one within the bounds of their places and callings, in the exercise of their gifts and graces) so the churches (when planted by the providence of God so as they may enjoy opportunity and advantage for it) ought to hold communion among themselves, for their peace, increase of love, and mutual edification. (Ephesians 6:18; Psalms 122:6; Romans 16:1, 2; 3 John 8-10)

15. In cases of difficulties or differences, either in point of doctrine or administration, wherein either the churches in general are concerned, or any one church, in their peace, union, and edification; or any member or members of any church are injured, in or by any proceedings in censures not agreeable to truth and order: it is according to the mind of Christ, that many churches holding communion together, do, by their messengers, meet to consider, and give their advice in or about that matter in difference, to be reported to all the churches concerned; howbeit these messengers assembled, are not intrusted with any church-power properly so called; or with any jurisdiction over the churches themselves, to exercise any censures either over any churches or persons; or to impose their determination on the churches or officers. (Acts 15:2, 4, 6, 22, 23, 25; 2 Corinthians 1:24; 1 John 4:1)

Chapter 27: Of the Communion of Saints

1. All saints that are united to Jesus Christ, their head, by his Spirit, and faith, although they are not made thereby one person with him, have fellowship in his graces, sufferings, death, resurrection, and glory; and, being united to one another in love, they have communion in each others gifts and graces, and are obliged to the performance of such duties, public and private, in an orderly way, as do conduce to their mutual good, both in the inward and outward man. (1 John 1:3; John 1:16; Philippians 3:10; Romans 6:5, 6; Ephesians 4:15, 16; 1 Corinthians 12:7; 1 Corinthians 3:21-23; 1

Thessalonians 5:11, 14; Romans 1:12; 1 John 3:17, 18; Galatians 6:10)

2. Saints by profession are bound to maintain an holy fellowship and communion in the worship of God, and in performing such other spiritual services as tend to their mutual edification; as also in relieving each other in outward things according to their several abilities, and necessities; which communion, according to the rule of the gospel, though especially to be exercised by them, in the relation wherein they stand, whether in families, or churches, yet, as God offereth opportunity, is to be extended to all the household of faith, even all those who in every place call upon the name of the Lord Jesus; nevertheless their communion one with another as saints, doth not take away or infringe the title or propriety which each man hath in his goods and possessions. (Hebrews 10:24, 25; Hebrews 3:12, 13; Acts 11:29, 30; Ephesians 6:4; 1 Corinthians 12:14-27; Acts 5:4; Ephesians 4:28)

Chapter 28: Of Baptism and the Lord's Supper

1. Baptism and the Lord's Supper are ordinances of positive and sovereign institution, appointed by the Lord Jesus, the only lawgiver, to be continued in his church to the end of the world. (Matthew 28:19, 20; 1 Corinthians 11:26)

2. These holy appointments are to be administered by those only who are qualified and thereunto called, according to the commission of Christ. (Matthew 28:19; 1 Corinthians 4:1)

Chapter 29: Of Baptism

1. Baptism is an ordinance of the New Testament, ordained by Jesus Christ, to be unto the party baptized, a sign of his fellowship with him, in his death and resurrection; of his being engrafted into him; of remission of sins; and of giving up into God, through Jesus Christ, to live and walk in newness of life. (Romans 6:3-5;

Colossians 2;12; Galatians 3:27; Mark 1:4; Acts 22:16; Romans 6:4)

2. Those who do actually profess repentance towards God, faith in, and obedience to, our Lord Jesus Christ, are the only proper subjects of this ordinance. (Mark 16:16; Acts 8:36, 37; Acts 2:41; Acts 8:12; Acts 18:8)

3. The outward element to be used in this ordinance is water, wherein the party is to be baptized, in the name of the Father, and of the Son, and of the Holy Spirit. (Matthew 28:19, 20; Acts 8:38)

4. Immersion, or dipping of the person in water, is necessary to the due administration of this ordinance. (Matthew 3:16; John 3:23)

Chapter 30: Of the Lord's Supper

1. The supper of the Lord Jesus was instituted by him the same night wherein he was betrayed, to be observed in his churches, unto the end of the world, for the perpetual remembrance, and shewing forth the sacrifice of himself in his death, confirmation of the faith of believers in all the benefits thereof, their spiritual nourishment, and growth in him, their further engagement in, and to all duties which they owe to him; and to be a bond and pledge of their communion with him, and with each other. (1 Corinthians 11:23-26; 1 Corinthians 10:16, 17, 21)

2. In this ordinance Christ is not offered up to his Father, nor any real sacrifice made at all for remission of sin of the quick or dead, but only a memorial of that one offering up of himself by himself upon the cross, once for all; and a spiritual oblation of all possible praise unto God for the same. So that the popish sacrifice of the mass, as they call it, is most abominable, injurious to Christ's own sacrifice the alone propitiation for all the sins of the elect. (Hebrews 9:25, 26, 28; 1 Corinthians 11:24; Matthew 26:26, 27)

3. The Lord Jesus hath, in this ordinance, appointed his ministers to pray, and bless the elements of bread and wine, and thereby to set them apart from a common to a holy use, and to take and break the bread; to take the cup, and, they communicating also themselves, to give both to the communicants. (1 Corinthians 11:23-26, etc.)

4. The denial of the cup to the people, worshipping the elements, the lifting them up, or carrying them about for adoration, and reserving them for any pretended religious use, are all contrary to the nature of this ordinance, and to the institution of Christ. (Matthew 26:26-28; Matthew 15:9; Exodus 20:4, 5)

5. The outward elements in this ordinance, duly set apart to the use ordained by Christ, have such relation to him crucified, as that truly, although in terms used figuratively, they are sometimes called by the names of the things they represent, to wit, the body and blood of Christ, albeit, in substance and nature, they still remain truly and only bread and wine, as they were before. (1 Corinthians 11:27; 1 Corinthians 11:26-28)

6. That doctrine which maintains a change of the substance of bread and wine, into the substance of Christ's body and blood, commonly called transubstantiation, by consecration of a priest, or by any other way, is repugnant not to Scripture alone, but even to common sense and reason, overthroweth the nature of the ordinance, and hath been, and is, the cause of manifold superstitions, yea, of gross idolatries. (Acts 3:21; Luke 24:6, 39; 1 Corinthians 11:24, 25)

7. Worthy receivers, outwardly partaking of the visible elements in this ordinance, do then also inwardly by faith, really and indeed, yet not carnally and corporally, but spiritually receive, and feed upon Christ crucified, and all the benefits of his death; the body and blood of Christ being then not corporally or carnally, but spiritually present to the faith of believers in that ordinance, as the elements themselves are to their outward senses. (1 Corinthians 10:16; 1

Corinthians 11:23-26)

8. All ignorant and ungodly persons, as they are unfit to enjoy communion with Christ, so are they unworthy of the Lord's table, and cannot, without great sin against him, while they remain such, partake of these holy mysteries, or be admitted thereunto; yea, whosoever shall receive unworthily, are guilty of the body and blood of the Lord, eating and drinking judgment to themselves. (2 Corinthians 6:14, 15; 1 Corinthians 11:29; Matthew 7:6)

Chapter 31: Of the State of Man after Death and Of the Resurrection of the Dead

1. The bodies of men after death return to dust, and see corruption; but their souls, which neither die nor sleep, having an immortal subsistence, immediately return to God who gave them. The souls of the righteous being then made perfect in holiness, are received into paradise, where they are with Christ, and behold the face of God in light and glory, waiting for the full redemption of their bodies; and the souls of the wicked are cast into hell; where they remain in torment and utter darkness, reserved to the judgment of the great day; besides these two places, for souls separated from their bodies, the Scripture acknowledgeth none. (Genesis 3:19; Acts 13:36; Ecclesiastes 12:7; Luke 23:43; 2 Corinthians 5:1, 6, 8; Philippians 1:23; Hebrews 12:23; Jude 6, 7; 1 Peter 3:19; Luke 16:23, 24)

2. At the last day, such of the saints as are found alive, shall not sleep, but be changed; and all the dead shall be raised up with the selfsame bodies, and none other; although with different qualities, which shall be united again to their souls forever. (1 Corinthians 15:51, 52; 1 Thessalonians 4:17; Job 19:26, 27; 1 Corinthians 15:42, 43)

3. The bodies of the unjust shall, by the power of Christ, be raised to dishonour; the bodies of the just, by his Spirit, unto honour, and be

made conformable to his own glorious body. (Acts 24:15; John 5:28, 29; Philippians 3:21)

Chapter 32: Of the Last Judgment

1. God hath appointed a day wherein he will judge the world in righteousness, by Jesus Christ; to whom all power and judgment is given of the Father; in which day, not only the apostate angels shall be judged, but likewise all persons that have lived upon the earth shall appear before the tribunal of Christ, to give an account of their thoughts, words, and deeds, and to receive according to what they have done in the body, whether good or evil. (Acts 17:31; John 5:22, 27; 1 Corinthians 6:3; Jude 6; 2 Corinthians 5:10; Ecclesiastes 12:14; Matthew 12:36; Romans 14:10, 12; Matthew 25:32-46)

2. The end of God's appointing this day, is for the manifestation of the glory of his mercy, in the eternal salvation of the elect; and of his justice, in the eternal damnation of the reprobate, who are wicked and disobedient; for then shall the righteous go into everlasting life, and receive that fulness of joy and glory with everlasting rewards, in the presence of the Lord; but the wicked, who know not God, and obey not the gospel of Jesus Christ, shall be cast aside into everlasting torments, and punished with everlasting destruction, from the presence of the Lord, and from the glory of his power. (Romans 9:22, 23; Matthew 25:21, 34; 2 Timothy 4:8; Matthew 25:46; Mark 9:48; 2 Thessalonians 1:7-10)

3. As Christ would have us to be certainly persuaded that there shall be a day of judgment, both to deter all men from sin, and for the greater consolation of the godly in their adversity, so will he have the day unknown to men, that they may shake off all carnal security, and be always watchful, because they know not at what hour the Lord will come, and may ever be prepared to say, Come Lord Jesus; come quickly. Amen. (2 Corinthians 5:10, 11; 2 Thessalonians 1:5-7; Mark 13:35-37; Luke 12:35-40; Revelation 22:20)

Closing Statement & Signatories

We the MINISTERS, and MESSENGERS of, and concerned for upwards of, one hundred BAPTIZED CHURCHES, in England and Wales (denying Arminianisim), being met together in London, from the third of the seventh month to the eleventh of the same, 1689, to consider of some things that might be for the glory of God, and the good of these congregations, have thought meet (for the satisfaction of all other Christians that differ from us in the point of Baptism) to recommend to their perusal the confession of our faith, which confession we own, as containing the doctrine of our faith and practice, and do desire that the members of our churches respectively do furnish themselves therewith.

Hansard Knollys, Pastor, Broken Wharf, London
William Kiffin, Pastor, Devonshire-square, London
John Harris, Pastor, Joiner's Hall, London
William Collins, Pastor, Petty France, London
Hurcules Collins, Pastor, Wapping, London
Robert Steed, Pastor, Broken Wharf, London
Leonard Harrison, Pastor, Limehouse, London
George Barret, Pastor, Mile End Green, London
Isaac Lamb, Pastor, Pennington-street, London
Richard Adams, Minister, Shad Thames, Southwark
Benjamin Keach, Pastor, Horse-lie-down, Southwark
Andrew Gifford, Pastor, Bristol, Frvars, Som. & Glouc.
Thomas Vaux, Pastor, Broadmead, Som. & Glouc.
Thomas Winnel, Pastor, Taunton, Som. & Glouc.
James Hitt, Preacher, Dalwood, Dorset
Richard Tidmarsh, Minister, Oxford City, Oxon
William Facey, Pastor, Reading, Berks
Samuel Buttall, Minister, Plymouth, Devon
Christopher Price, Minister, Abergayenny, Monmouth
Daniel Finch, Minister, Kingsworth, Herts
John Ball, Tiverton, Devon
Edmond White, Pastor, Evershall, Bedford
William Prichard, Pastor, Blaenau, Monmouth

Paul Fruin, Minister, Warwick, Warwick
Richard Ring, Pastor, Southhampton, Hants
John Tomkins, Minister, Abingdon, Berks
Toby Willes, Pastor, Bridgewater, Somerset
John Carter, Steventon, Bedford
James Webb, Devizes, Wilts
Richard Sutton, Pastor, Tring, Herts
Robert Knight, Pastor, Stukeley, Bucks
Edward Price, Pastor, Hereford City, Hereford
William Phipps, Pastor, Exon, Devon
William Hawkins, Pastor, Dimmock, Gloucester
Samuel Ewer, Pastor, Hemstead, Herts
Edward Man, Pastor, Houndsditch, London
Charles Archer, Pastor, Hock-Norton, Oxon
In the name of and on the behalf of the whole assembly.

Notes:

1. Taken from Expository Apologetics by Voddie Baucham Jr., © 2015, pp. 30. Used by permission of Crossway, a publishing ministry of Good News Publishers, Wheaton, IL 60187, www.crossway.org.

2. Taken from Family Shepherds by Voddie Baucham Jr., © 2011, pp. 71. Used by permission of Crossway, a publishing ministry of Good News Publishers, Wheaton, IL 60187, www.crossway.org.

54390296R00130

Made in the USA
San Bernardino, CA
16 October 2017